ISBN : 0-9689781-1-8
Legal Deposit – Bibliothèque nationale du Québec, 2002
Legal Deposit – National Library of Canada, 2002

Published by:
Les Aliments Massawippi inc.
North Hatley (Quebec)
J0B 2C0 Canada
massawippi@globetrotter.net

PRINTED IN CANADA

"I feel that miso soup is the most essential part of a person's diet… I have found that, with very few exceptions, families which make a practice of serving miso soup daily are almost never sick… By enjoying miso soup each day, your constitution will gradually improve and you will develop resistance to disease. I believe that miso belongs to the highest class of medicines, those which help prevent disease and strengthen the body through continued usage."

Dr. Shinichiro Akizuki,
Director, Saint Francis Hospital , Nagasaki,
Japan, 1965 and 1972, cited in Shurtleff
and Aoyagi's The Book of Miso, 1983.

Contents

ACKNOWLEDGEMENTS 1
ABOUT THE AUTHOR 2
INTRODUCTION 3

WHAT IS MISO? 5
THE ART OF MAKING MISO 6
EXCEPTIONAL NUTRITIVE QUALITIES 7
    A Few of the Benefits of Fermentation 8
    Ideal Ingredient in Weight-Loss Diets 8
NON-PASTEURIZED MISO: A LIVING FOOD 9
    The Importance of Enzymes 9
    The Three Main Enzyme Groups 11
    Miso, a Functional Food with Probiotic Organisms 12
MISO, PROVIDER OF PHYSICAL WELL-BEING, HEALING AND
LONGEVITY AGENT 14
    Anti-radiation and Antitoxin 14
    Antioxidant 14
    Prevention of Cardiovascular Diseases 15
    Prevention and Treatment of Cancer 16
    Alleviation of the Symptoms of Menopause 17
    Reduced Allergic Reaction and Food Intolerance 17
    Easing of Gastric Problems and their Symptoms 18
    Prevention of Hypertension 19
    Increased Longevity 19
    Anti-Pathogenic and Healing Qualities 19
THE IMPACT OF GMOs ON HEALTH 20
WHY EAT ORGANIC FOOD? 22

ENTREES 25
    Miso Melitzanosalata (pureed eggplant) 26
    Guacamole 27
    Miso Sushi 28
    Vegetarian Pâté 29
    Spring Rolls 30

BROTHS AND SOUPS 33
    Simple and Delicious Miso Broth 34
    Miso Consommé 35
    Cream of Leek Soup 36
    Oriental Meal Soup 37
    Vegetarian Goulash 38
    Onion Soup au Gratin 39

SALADS 41
  Greek Style Bean Salad 42
  Fusilli Salad with Tuna 43
  Oriental Salad 44

MAIN DISHES 45
  Fresh Tomato Pasta 46
  Vegetarian Pasta 47
  Ibishyimbo (kidney beans) with Tomatoes and Sunflower Seeds 48
  Japanese Salmon Steak 49
  Tofu Croquettes with Miso 50
  Singhalese Rice 52
  Dhal (lentils) 53

VEGETABLES AND SIDE DISHES 55
  Green Beans with Sesame Oil and Garlic 56
  African Spinach 57
  Miso Ibitoke (plantains or cooking bananas) 58
  Miso Corn 59
  Ratatouille 60

SAUCES AND VINAIGRETTES 61
  Dijon Mustard Vinaigrette 62
  Mayonnaise Vinaigrette 63
  Yogurt and Honey Vinaigrette 63
  Peanut Sauce 64
  Aïoli Sauce 65
  Miso Barbecue Sauce 65
  Marinade for Brochettes 66
  Sweet and Sour Miso Marinade 67

OTHER USEFUL RECIPES 69
  Broth for Infants 70
  Soy Milk 71
  Soy Yogurt 72
  Germination 73
  Making Pasta (Simple and Easy) 74
  Chapati (unleavened bread) 75
  Healthy Baked Beans (with no Fat) 76
  More Digestible Milk 77
  Sauerkraut and Lacto-Fermentation 78

Bibliography 80

A c k n o w l e d g e m e n t s

I wish to begin by thanking Gilbert, my life companion and partner, for his humour, his support and assistance in the creation of this cookbook. Many thanks as well go to all those individuals, friends and collaborators, who actively worked at compiling the recipes as we all worked at finding ways to incorporate miso into our respective cooking habits. A very special thank you goes to Nada Terzic Stevanovic who agreed to test many of the recipes.

Thank you to Francine Masson, marketing counsellor for the Canadian Technology Network, for her judicious advice regarding book content and presentation. She wisely insisted that the book be enhanced with illustrations.

Thank you to Canada Economic Development who granted us a loan to market our products and made publishing this book a reality.

Suzanne Dionne

About the Author

Suzanne Dionne, the sixth child in a family of 14, is a food professional and a graduate from Laval University (Quebec) in the early 1980's.

Having spent five years as a researcher at the Centre de nutrition of Laval University (Quebec), Suzanne then travelled to Central Africa where she lived for a number of years. While there, she worked in nutrition centres and introduced techniques for preparing health products (soy milk, basic foods, cereals for infants). As well, she counselled various women's groups and launched small food-processing businesses (miso, baked goods, tofu, breakfast cereals, etc.).

Suzanne returned to Quebec and with her husband settled in the Eastern Townships, with the goal of establishing an organic food-processing business based on the research and development of natural and organic health products.

In October 1999, with a Masters degree in business administration, she put together her business plan. Les Aliments Massawippi inc. opened for business in January 2000; miso was produced, a laboratory was set up and final touches were made on other products designed to improve health. In June 2001, Suzanne received the Prix Entrepreneurship féminin at the Concours québécois en entrepreneurship 2001.

Her goal has always been to maintain and improve one's health in terms of how food is processed and prepared.

At last, a cookbook totally devoted to miso that extends far beyond cooking because miso is much more than food. The delicious fermented soy paste, based on thousand-year-old techniques of preparation in Asia, is similar in taste to beef and chicken concentrates yet is entirely vegetable based. One acquires a taste for miso as for good wines and cheeses, which are produced much the same way as miso.

Bad eating habits, conveniently maintained by a food industry that has little regard for nature, continue to dominate the Western World. Non-pasteurized organic miso can both counter the trend and enhance food, without GMOs.

Non-pasteurized miso is a living food that contains lactobacilli, enzymes and other micro-organisms beneficial to the body. Lactobacilli protect against pathogenic organisms (*E. coli* bacteria, salmonella, *Shigella*). Enzymes enhance digestion and the assimilation of nutrients. Miso helps reduce symptoms related to digestion such as acidity, ulcers, Crohn's disease, constipation, lactose, starch and gluten intolerance, and food allergies. Other components such as lecithin, linoleic acid and isoflavones help maintain a healthy cholesterol level.

Extensive research in many parts of Asia and the United States has led researchers to uncover the health benefits of constituents of miso. Other examples: soy isoflavones can play a major role in preventing cardiovascular disease and some types of cancers and in reducing certain symptoms of menopause; tests also indicate that a daily consumption of two cups of miso broth constitutes adequate protection against hypertension. Miso is a functional food with preventive and curative properties. It can be said with certainty that miso helps maintain and improve vitality.

Miso contains no cholesterol, is low in fat, and includes multiple complex B vitamins and all the essential amino acids, those not produced by the body alone but indispensable to maintaining good health.

This book is a journey of discovery of international dishes creatively and tastefully adapted by the author to include miso. Some recipes are her own while others are classic dishes from around the world.

The cookbook includes forty recipes, from entrees to main dishes, soups, salads and side dishes. They are easy to prepare, delicious, with familiar tastes or tastes to discover, and include useful recipes for particular diets, child nutrition or simply the preparation of basic ingredients.

Almost all recipes in this book require no salt as miso is salty to the taste. In fact, miso generally works well as a substitute for salt in most recipes. As you become familiar with the recipes, you will discover the versatility of miso as an ingredient in your food preparation. Let your imagination flow, improvise, experiment, create and enjoy.

A final note. Avoid cooking non-pasteurized miso, if possible, to preserve its maximum health benefits. It is therefore preferable to add it at the end of the cooking process or to the prepared dish.

Bon Appétit ...To Your Health!

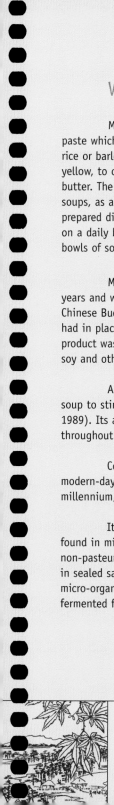

What is Miso?

Miso (pronounced "meeso" in Japan) is a savoury fermented paste which is high in protein and made of soy beans, cereal such as rice or barley, water, and salt. Its color can vary from cream or pale yellow, to chocolate brown and its texture resembles that of peanut butter. The comparison ends there. Miso can be used as a seasoning for soups, as a base for making a broth or sauce and as an ingredient in prepared dishes; it is also a wonderful meat substitute. It can be eaten on a daily basis, in amounts of 20 g or so per person, equivalent to two bowls of soup a day (Steinkraus, 1983).

Miso, or chiang, has been a staple in China for approximately 2,500 years and was introduced in Japan in the 7th Century, in all probability by a Chinese Buddhist priest. In the 8th Century, the imperial court of Japan already had in place a food safety department where miso played a major role. The food product was included in the wages for government officials along with rice, salt, soy and other types of beans and grains.

Approximately 75% of the Japanese population starts its day with miso soup to stimulate and energise, without the side effects of coffee (Monette, 1989). Its alkaline content stimulates the mind and body while providing energy throughout the morning hours.

Considering the increasing importance given to soy-based foods in modern-day nutrition, it can be said that miso is the Bovril of the new millennium, its taste and use being similar to the famous broth.

It is important to note that in order to derive all of the health benefits found in miso, it must not be purchased in pasteurized form — the words non-pasteurized or unpasteurized should appear on the product label. Miso sold in sealed sachets is pasteurized: the enzymes, lactobacilli and other friendly micro-organisms have been lost in the process. Finally, miso that has been fermented for a long time can be kept in the refrigerator for months, even years.

The Art of Making Miso

Miso is the result of double fermentation. Cereal, a starchy base as from rice or barley, is steamed to obtain the optimal humidity needed for the culture to grow. The grains are inoculated with strains of Aspergillus oryzae and lactobacilli, then left to ferment for approximately 45 hours, until each grain is coated with a white mycelium and yields what is known as koji. The first fermentation requires specific conditions: heat, humidity and an aerobic environment - the presence of oxygen. Following the first fermentation, the koji is combined with other ingredients, is crushed and undergoes a second fermentation. This must be done under anaerobic conditions — in an air-tight environment.

It takes three days to complete the initial processing stages before the miso is placed in a vat for the second fermentation, which can last from one week up to two or even three years, depending on the type of miso required. Miso comes in many varieties. The production of miso dates back to a complex art form as important in Asia as the production of cheese and wine in the Western World (Monette, 1989).

How miso is made

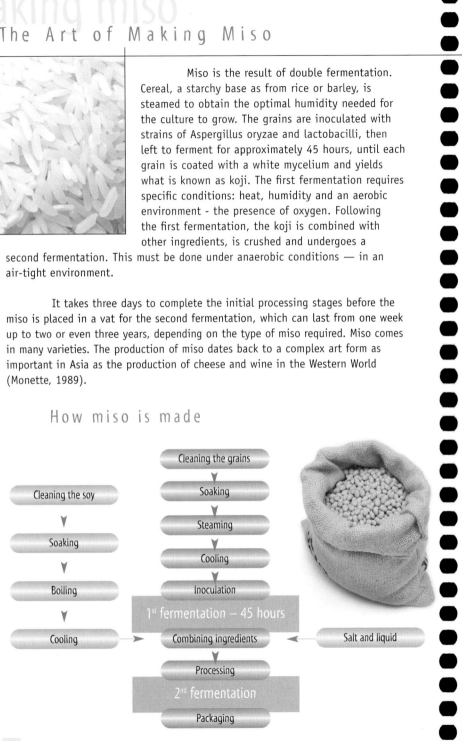

Cleaning the grains
↓
Soaking
↓
Steaming
↓
Cooling
↓
Inoculation
↓
1st fermentation – 45 hours

Cleaning the soy
↓
Soaking
↓
Boiling
↓
Cooling
→

Combining ingredients ← Salt and liquid
↓
Processing
↓
2nd fermentation
↓
Packaging

Exceptional Nutritive Qualities

The main ingredient in miso is soy (or soya in Europe), a leguminous plant that originated in Asia 3,000 years ago. As such, miso is a principal source of protein in a diet, along with other leguminous sources, tofu, nuts and grains, fish and sea food, eggs, chicken, dairy products and meat.

Miso production is based on enzymatic hydrolysis which makes it possible to break down complex molecules into simple molecules. For example, soy and added cereal proteins (rice or barley) are broken down into amino acids and low-density peptides, making them more digestible and more easily assimilated. The same applies to carbohydrates, lipids and other nutrients.

In addition to tasting good, miso contains all of the essential amino acids, making it a complete source of protein that rivals sources of animal protein. Amino acids in miso are well balanced as proteins from soy and rice are complementary: lysine, abundant in soy, completes a cereal such as rice which contains little of it. Its high nutritive value stems also from its vitamin B content and minerals (see the following table).

Nutritional Analysis of Hatcho* Miso

	Water	Energy	Proteins	Lipids	Total Carbohydrates	Fibre
Per 100g of Miso	40 %	224 cal	21 g	10,2 g	12 g	1,8 g

	Calcium	Phosphor	Iron	Vit A	Vit B1	Vit B2	Niacin
Per 100g of Miso	154 mg	264 mg	7,1 mg	0 U.I.	0,04 mg	0,13 mg	1,3 mg

*Variety of Miso
Source: Standard tables of food composition, Japan

In general, 60% of lipids found in miso are polyunsaturated fats, 20% are monounsaturated, and only 20% are saturated fats. Miso contains no cholesterol and its lecithin content can even control the level of cholesterol.

All the more interesting and important in modern-day diets, non-pasteurized miso enhances food digestion and assimilation. A product of solid fermentation, it contains micro-organisms and fifty different enzymes, all beneficial for the body.

A Few of the Benefits of Fermentation

Vitamin deficiency, not a rare occurrence in modern-day diets, can be remedied two ways: by grain germination and by fermentation. Micro-organisms synthesise group B vitamins and, at times, vitamin C.

Soy that has fermented for a period of 40 hours clearly has a higher vitamin content than unfermented soy, as the following table illustrates.

Vitamin Content in Fermented Soy Compared to Unfermented Soy (Aubert, 1985)

Vitamin	Increase (number of times)
Riboflavin (vitamin B2)	2 to 47 times
Niacin (PP factor)	2 to 5 times
Pyridoxine (vitamin B6)	4 to 14 times
Biotin	2 to 3 times
Vitamin B12	33 times
Pantothenic acid (vitamin B5)	2 to 4 times

As a fermented food enhances the effect of lactic intestinal flora, the latter synthesises vitamin B1 (thiamine) in greater quantities. The same applies to rice fermented with leguminous plants which synthesises vitamins B1, B2 and PP, as is the case for miso.

Finally, fermenting and cooking break down the anti-nutritional factors naturally present in soy such as the inhibitor of trypsin, hemagglutinins and phytic acid[1].

Ideal Ingredient in Weight-Loss Diets

Miso is a hypocaloric type of food. It is low in fat and generally contains no more than 27 calories per tablespoon. It is therefore ideal for individuals who want to lose weight. Its proteins provide a heightened sense of being full, which helps absorb fewer calories without feeling hungry (Cyr, June 30, 2001). Also, glucose resulting from fermentation and soon assimilated after the intake, promptly alleviates hunger pangs.

---

[1] *This acid combines in the organism with calcium, iron, magnesium and zinc to form insoluble phytates eliminated by the organism. According to some authors, the elimination could cause a demineralization in individuals who eat a lot of whole grain cereals, in which phytic acid was not broken down.*

Non-Pasteurized Miso:
a Living Food

As part of a healthy diet, the importance of eating fresh and nutritious foods is increasingly well known. The benefits of fermented foods such as yogurt, miso and lacto-fermented vegetables for body and health are also recognised.

The Importance of Enzymes

The presence of high amounts of enzymes in fresh foods breaks down complex molecules into more easily digested simple molecules. For example, lipases help digest fats and absorb the fat soluble vitamins (vitamins A, D, E, K and all carotenes), while amylases help break down carbohydrates (sugar and starch). Nature has made it such that enzymes naturally present in food help digestion rather than leave the task to enzymes found in the body. Unfortunately, most foods have undergone some form of heat process (cooking, pasteurisation or other types of sterilisation), and enzymes are sensitive to heat.

The addition of vegetable enzymes to a diet enhances digestion. Their role is all the more important for older people whose enzyme activity is weaker, leading to a lack or shortage of enzymes and provoking digestive problems such as colic, flatulence, hyperacidity and various forms of food intolerance. Several enzyme deficiencies are clearly connected to an inability to digest food properly; for example, a lack of lactase causes lactose intolerance (LactAid, 1960). A number of benefits attributed to fermented vegetable enzymes taken orally have been noted, as in cases of anorexia, chronic gastroenteritis, dyspepsia, etc. (Reed, 1977; Shurtleff, 1983). Also, enzymes from vegetables are often activated at pH levels and stages of the digestion process when body enzymes have stopped having an effect (see frame). As such, it is not only beneficial but essential to select foods containing enzymes in order for the digestion process to be as complete and efficient as possible as these enzymes act at much higher pH concentrations and are reliable (Cyr, April 21, 2001). The addition of fermented enzymes enhances food digestion and decreases related digestive problems (Hesseltine, 1965).

The Tanaka's Experiment

Cited in Reed (1977), the Tanaka's experiment illustrates how enzymes found in foods complement enzymes produced by the body during the digestion process. The experiment is conducted on human gastric juices with and without added Aspergillus oryzae enzymes, the same micro-organism found in miso.

The pH level in gastric juices is between 1.5 and 2.2 before a meal, 4.0 and 5.0 within 30 minutes following the meal, 2.0 and 4.5 within 60 minutes after the meal, and between 1.5 and 2.0 following the complete digestion process. It is known that the enzyme effect is a function of the existing pH level. Tests have indicated that pectic enzyme activity is at its highest at a very low pH level. However, at a pH level of 2.2 and higher, more than half of the proteolytic activity is due to Aspergillus oryzae protease. Pepsin activity diminishes considerably when at a pH level beyond 3.5. That is when amylase from the salivary glands is activated. At a pH level of approximately 4.5, the salivary amylase becomes almost inactive while that from Aspergillus oryzae is very active. Enzymes from Aspergillus oryzae play a role at all stages of digestion.

Source: REED, Gerald, Enzymes in food processing, Academic Press, New York, 1977, 409 pp.

The incorporation of supplemental enzymes in a diet is common throughout the world and more particularly in France and Japan. In Japan, commercially available digestive enzymes are made from the same strains used to make miso (Reed, 1977). In the United States, in 1970, Aspergillus oryzae was used to make alpha-amylase, pectinase, protease, adenylic deaminase acid, amylase, lactase, invertase, protease acids and cellulase (Blain, 1975; Moo-Young, 1982; Steinkraus, 1982). In Canada, digestion enhancing enzymes, classified by Health Canada under medication or drugs, usually come in capsule or pill form.

All of the above enzymes are found in miso. Some fifty enzymes have been found in koji (Bienvenido, 1985), the product of the first fermentation in the production of miso. The main enzymes released by koji are protease, amylase and lipase (Arima, 1967; Sakurai, 1977) and, overall, Aspergillus oryzae displays a high lipolytic activity (Yeoh, 1986).

The Three Main Enzyme Groups

Proteases are enzymes that break proteins down into their original components, amino acids, which can then be absorbed through the intestinal wall.

The improper digestion of proteins can lead to problems such as food allergies, bowel irritation, skin problems such as psoriasis, some forms of toxicity, etc.

Protease play a protective role in eliminating yeast in the small intestine thus helping prevent candidiasis and the onset of harmful bacteria, protozoa and other parasites.

Amylases are a group of enzymes that hydrolyse carbohydrates (starch and other complex sugars) into basic sugars (various dextrin, maltose, fructose, dextrose, glucose, etc.). For example, lactase hydrolyses lactose into glucose and galactose, while maltase breaks down maltose into two glucose molecules. The latter is the most basic of sugar molecules, making it the most easily assimilated.

Lipases are enzymes capable of breaking down fat by releasing fatty acids. Their role in helping digest fat makes them essential to controlling the level of cholesterol.

Miso, a Functional Food with Probiotic Organisms

A functional food is a food or ingredient that, beyond its basic nutritional value, is known to enhance health or exhibit preventive or curative qualities. As such, miso may be called a functional food.

Lactobacilli and other micro-organisms found in miso are probiotiocs, bacteria that have a positive effect on health and well-being by way of bioactive substances such as enzymes, or by way of positive effects on the intestinal microflora. Probiotic micro-organisms nourish the good bacteria in the intestine (Cyr, April 21, 2001). By clear definition, probiotics positively enhance the composition of the flora in various ways, thus offering advantages like (Klaenhammer, 2000):

- anti-pathogenic blocking, elimination and counter properties;

- immuno-stimulation and immuno-modulation;

- anti-cancerous and anti-mutagenic effects;

- relief from lactose intolerance symptoms;

- reduction of the incidence of diarrhea (associated with taking antibiotics, with *Clostridium difficile*, travelling abroad and rotaviruses);

- prevention of vaginitis;

- healthy mucous membranes.

Probiotics have additional positive effects on health. A summary of the book by Chaitow and Trenev (1990) lists these health benefits:

- They manufacture B-vitamins, such as biotin, niacin (B3), pyridoxine (B6) and folic acid.

- They act as anti-carcinogenic (anti-cancer) factors, with powerful anti-tumour potentials.

- They act as 'watchdogs' by keeping an eye on, and effectively controlling, the spread of undesirable micro-organisms (by altering the acidity of the region they inhabit and/or producing specific antibiotic substances, as well as by depriving rival unfriendly bacteria of their nutrients). The antibiotics some of the friendly bacteria produce are effective against many harmful bacteria, viruses and fungi. Not the least of the potentially harmful yeasts controlled by some lactobacilli is "Candida albicans," now implicated in many health problems in people who are malnourished or whose immune systems are depleted.

- They effectively help to control high cholesterol levels.

- They sometimes act to relieve the symptoms of anxiety.

- They play a role in protecting against the negative effects of radiation and toxic pollutants, enhancing immune function.

- They help considerably to enhance bowel function.

- They help to raise the level of oestrogen in women, thus decreasing the symptoms of menopause.

For more information:
http://www.holisticmed.com/detox/dtx-probio.txt

CHAITOW, Leon et Natasha TRENEV. Probiotics
Thorsons Publishing Group, Northamptonshire, England, 1990

Miso, Provider of Physical Well-Being, Healing and Longevity Agent

"May thy food be thy medicine" declared Hippocrates, the father of Western medicine, more than two millennia ago.

Miso has undeniable health benefits; its various components have been the subject of endless research in countries around the world. These components will be discussed, in the following paragraphs, in terms of how miso and good health go together.

Anti-radiation and Antitoxin

Miso helps the body counter the effects of pollution and helps prevent diseases caused by radioactivity (Akizuki, 1965-72 and Morishita, 1972, cited in Shurtleff, 1983). In 1972, it was discovered that miso contains dipicolinic acid, an alkaloid capable of eliminating heavy metals from the body. As such, it is effective in countering the side effects of radiation therapy in patients suffering from cancer.

Generally speaking, people who live in industrialised nations consume too many acidic foods and too few alkaline foods. As such, a decrease of the pH level in the cells of the body makes their membranes less permeable, and the consequences are two-fold: nutrients are less efficiently absorbed and body waste is more difficult to expel from the cells. As a result, energy levels are reduced and the body functions less efficiently (Cyr, 1999). Consequences can lead to degenerative diseases such as osteo-porosis, cancer, fibromyalgia, arthritis, fatigue and problems of the immune system.

Antioxidant

Free radicals are highly reactive molecules that may cause oxidative damages to the cells. It is a well-known scientific fact that the excessive production of free radicals can provoke a number of illnesses such as Behcet disease, Crohn's disease, colitis, herpes, neutrophilic lymphocite, etc. It has been noted that toxic agents such as paraquat (a herbicide), insecticides, nitrogen oxyde (produced by vehicles) and ultraviolet rays produce free radicals. Again, they are linked to various illnesses: malignant tumours, serious topical forms of dermatitis together with forms of retinitis, cataracts, skin cancer, male sterility, fibrosis, etc.

Miso is popular for its content in isoflavones, antioxidants that resemble oestrogens.

The fermentation of rice and soy by Aspergillus oryzae has the particular effect of releasing high amounts of isoflavones, light molecular-weight components. Thus, miso can play an intrinsic role in defense against oxidative ailments, together with other low-molecular-weight antioxidants such as vitamin C, E and A, polyphenols, catechu (tannin found in tea and red wine) and flavonoids (Niwa, Y., 1999).

Prevention of Cardiovascular Diseases

Phytosterols are lipid (sterol) organic (phyto) compounds naturally found in plants. So far, more than 40 studies have indicated that a diet high in phytosterols reduces the level of cholesterol and low-density lipoproteins (LDL, also known as "bad cholesterol") and, as such, the risk of heart disease (Landry, 2000). Soy is an important source of phytosterols, as are vegetable oils, nuts and sesame and sunflower seeds.

Omega-3 types of fatty acids have been the subject of widespread research. It is now known that this type of fatty acid helps reduce the level of triglycerides (Landry, 2000). Omega-3 are found mainly in fish (tuna, bass, sardines, mackerel and salmon). Other good sources of omega-3 are flax, soy, green leafy vegetables, nuts and tofu. Miso is made from whole soy beans, making it another good source of omega-3.

Miso also contains complex B vitamins. A number of studies indicate that blood with a moderately high homocysteine content has a strong negative effect on the lining of the blood vessels and on the progressive blocking of the arteries. Complex B vitamins (B6, B12 and folic acid) act as homocysteine blood serum stabilisers. There are various sources of vitamin B: liver, green leafy vegetables, legumes, cooked wheat germ, soy flour, yeast, and enriched breads and cereals.

Research shows that people who consume high quantities of food rich in phyto-chemical components are less prone to heart disease. Like vitamin B, phyto-chemical components help reduce the level of bad cholesterol (LDL) and of triglycerides. Phyto-chemical compounds include carotenoids (tomatoes and their composites, red or orange-coloured vegetables, watermelon, guava and pink grapefruit), flavonoids (green or black tea, onions, broccoli and red wine), and isoflavones (miso, soy milk and flour, tofu and cooked soybeans).

The U.S. Food and Drug Administration (FDA) recognises that consuming soy helps reduce the risk of heart disease. As part of a diet low in saturated fat and cholesterol, soy can reduce the overall level of cholesterol, the level of bad cholesterol (LDL), and increase the level of good cholesterol (HDL). The FDA recommends the daily consumption of 25 g of soy protein for effectiveness (Landry, 2001).

Because it is rich in lecithin and linoleic acid, miso is important in controlling cholesterol levels.

Prevention and Treatment of Cancer

Major research has been conducted on the anti-cancerous properties of miso, notably in Japan and the United States. It is known that the daily consumption of miso will reduce the incidence of gastric cancer by 33% (Shurtleff, 1982; Hirayama, 1981, cited in Shurtleff, 1983).

Miso is also a strong antioxidant (Yamaguchi, 1979, cited in Ebine, 1989). As with Vitamins C and E, miso prevents the oxidation of foods and, as such, the forming of free radicals, making it effective in preventing some types of cancers and heart diseases.

Isoflavones such as genistein and daidzein can play an important role in preventive medicine, notably in the prevention of cancer. Isoflavones are anti-cancer metabolites, destroying or hindering the growth of cancerous cells (Kaufman et al., 1997). Miso is an excellent source of genistein and daidzein. Scientific experiments have indicated that isoflavones in miso are capable of breaking down radicals (antiradical properties) the same way as alpha-tocopherol (vitamin E). Genistein has demonstrated a strong capacity to limit the proliferation of acute leukemia (Hirota et al., 2000).

Research among Japanese middle-age women has indicated that isoflavones in their diet come mostly from miso, tofu and natto (fermented and glutinous soybeans) (Arai Y. et al., 2000).

Miso also contains melanoidins, groups of plant melanin that tend to prevent the growth of cancer cells (Kamei, H. et al., 1997). It can act as a chemical blocking agent in colon cancer (Masaoka et al., 1998). Also, it has been clearly demonstrated that the daily intake of miso soup significantly reduced the risk of stomach cancer (Hirayama, 1982).

Research also indicates that miso is effective in preventing breast cancer. It has a potential anti-tumour effect when combined with tamoxifen, a component in the treatment of breast cancer (Gotoh et al., 1998).

Considering equal amounts of NaCl (table salt), the incidence of cancer has been shown to be lower in people who get their salt from miso (Watanabe et al., 1999).

Alleviation of the Symptoms of Menopause

Recent research seems to indicate that the regular intake of soy helps reduce the symptoms of menopause (hot flashes, night sweats, headaches and insomnia), decreases the risk of developing certain types of cancer (breast, prostate and colon), controls the level of glycemia in people with diabetes and reduces the risk of osteoporosis and kidney stones (Landry, 2001).

Reduced Allergic Reaction and Food Intolerance

A study in Japan has shown that 80% of people allergic to soy have no allergic reaction to miso, a hypo-allergenic food product. Enzymes found in miso make it possible for people who eat it to overcome allergies (Ogawa, Samoto and Takahashi, 2000). For example, lactase developed by Aspergillus orizae, the strain used to produce miso, can render milk tolerable for people who are usually lactose intolerant.

Miso also helps maintain intestinal flora, increasing it and regulating the functions of the stomach and intestine. Miso is well recommended for people suffering from digestive problems or food intolerance.

17

Alkaline Foods

All vegetables, all fruits (except for cranberries), sprouts, algae, spirulina, lean chicken breast, farm eggs, tofu, flax, squash, sunflower or pumpkin seeds, millet, (the only alkaline cereal), cider vinegar, green tea, spices, organic milk (non-pasteurized), miso, tamari and aromatic herbs.

Acidic Foods

All oils, all cereals such as wheat, rice, barley, buckwheat, etc, (except millet), cranberries, cheeses (goat, sheep, cow), milk, butter, animal proteins (beef, fish, sea food, wild game), pasta, legumes, potatoes, yeast in beer, soy milk, nuts, sweets and sweeteners, medicines, chemical products and alcoholic beverages.

Source: CYR, Josiane. « Eau pétillante sucrée : pas si naturelle », Les Conseils de Josiane, La Bonne Table, section I, Le Soleil, January 27, 2001, p. 8.

Easing of Gastric Problems and their Symptoms

What we eat largely influences normal body functions. One consequence is body acidity or alkalinity. Diets in the Western world are often too high in acids which makes it more difficult to expel waste from our cells and slows down the absorption of nutrients (Cyr, January 27, 2001).

The high buffer potential of miso makes it favourable in maintaining a pH[2] level in the stomach when combined with other foods (Ebine, 1989), and reduces the incidence of gastro-intestinal problems (ulcers, burning sensation, colon irritation, etc.) linked to excess acidity.

---

[2] *pH (hydrogen power) is the unit of measure for acidity or alkalinity in a given milieu. The pH can vary from 0 to 14. A pH of 7 is neutral. The lower the pH (ex. 1.0) the more acidic the milieu. The higher the pH level, the more alkaline the milieu. The normal human body pH level is about 7 (except for the stomach with a pH level from 1 to 4.5).*

Prevention of Hypertension

Consuming at least two bowls of miso soup daily provides adequate protection against hypertension (Kanda A. et al., 1999), even though miso is a salty food.

Increased Longevity

The island of Okinawa, in Japan, has the strongest concentration of 100-year-old people in the world. Experts who have studied the people of the region have observed that their diet is highly vegetarian, low in salt, high in carbohydrates and moderate in proteins. A daily menu includes miso soup, dry algae and rice for breakfast, and a mixture of tofu or soy protein, rice products and vegetables at other meals (Walker, 2001).

Anti-Pathogenic and Healing Qualities

Studies suggest that probiotic bacteria such as lactobacilli can curb the excessive growth of disease-causing organisms whether they are bacterial, viral or fungal, and of disease-causing germs such as salmonella, *Shigella, Campylobacter* and some strains of *E. coli*. It can truthfully be said that probiotic bacteria are effective weapons for preventing and treating microbial infections (Roy, 2000). Just thinking about the contaminated drinking water in Walkerton and the "hamburger sickness", it is reassuring to know that prevention and protection are available in the form of a living food.

Considering its content in probiotic organisms and its exceptional nutritional qualities, miso is the obvious food choice for people during convalescence. Nutritionists in hospitals would do well to make widespread use of miso for patients. Hospitalised patients would be getting a food that would speed up their recovery time while protecting them against disease causing germs and infections during a period when they are weak and more vulnerable.

Genetically modified organisms (GMO) are species, plant or animal, which have been altered with one or more foreign genes (from another species, or bacteria or virus) to provide them with characteristics not found in the species natural state. They are as such laboratory specimens, not products of nature.

Should we turn a blind eye to science? Genes or synthetic DNA fragments transferred with methods established during the last 20 years are well-known to geneticists who manipulate them; they are often synthetic genetic assembling made from the DNA of various organisms (virus, bacteria, plant or animal). That is not the case for the genetic (hereditary) material of a plant or animal, about which little is known, and into which the fragments are transferred. Transgenic fragments haphazardly implant themselves into the chromosomes of cells which then regenerate a given organism to found a new subspecies (Séralini, 2000), where it is little known if the chemical properties will be in harmony with nature.

According to Bernard Herzog[3], French microbiologist and doctor of nutrition therapy, foreign genes introduced into plants do not conform with metabolic cells which, consequently, do not recognise them. Their effect will be to overcharge the immune system with a group of inactive molecules. With regard to human genome and organs this can provoke a series of mutations which can make them vulnerable to bacteria and new strains of viruses (Herzog, 2000, cited in Pilon, 2001). In his daily practice, Doctor Herzog noticed that some bacteria had undergone so many mutations that treatment with antibiotics had become ineffective. In Europe, there has been a multitude of allergies and illnesses of the immune system in young people since the introduction of genetically altered foods.

Many serious illnesses untreatable with conventional medicine can be successfully treated with a change of diet insofar as, according to Herzog, they are connected to food containing GMOs: thrombocytopenia, lung infections due to a weak immune system, bone loss, lymphomas, endometriosis, uterine cancer.

A number of extreme cases could be treated by eliminating genetically modified manufactured products from the diet and by consuming natural products rich in vitamins: fruits, vegetables, whole grain cereals and legumes. Yves Gagnon (2001) states that organic products are the only counter measure against GMOs.

---

[3] HERZOG, Bernard. Le transgénique : les premiers signes d'une catastrophe, Les Éditions du CRAM, Collection Santé et Alimentation, Montréal, 2000, 300p. This book is largely cited in the special issue on GMOs of Bio-Bulle, the Quebec magazine on organic food and agriculture, n° 31, june 2001, p. 22-23.

According to Agriculture Canada[4], approximately 70% of processed foods can contain GMOs. It is difficult to avoid eating GMOs unless a label states all ingredients in a given product. Under these conditions, a food type such as organic non-pasteurized miso can help counter the negative effects of GMOs by fighting allergies, improving the immune system and helping the digestive system expel unwanted elements.

For more information:

http://www.greenmoney.com/gmj/sum00/sum600.htm
http://www.identigen.com/html2/MainBgL.htm
http://www.centerforfoodsafety.org/
http://www.newscientist.com/hottopics/gm/
http://www.thecampaign.org/
http://bam.tao.ca/en/whatdo/accueil.htm
http://www.cab.qc.ca/dossiers.htm

[4] The list of products manufacturers state have no GMOs or could contain GMOs, on the website of Biotech Action Montréal: http://bam.tao.ca/en/whatdo/accueil.htm

organic food

A healthy soil is the basis for organic farming. Those who practice this type of farming choose plants and animals adapted to their environment. To create an ecologically stable farming environment, rotation is essential combined with natural methods of fertilising and enriching the soil, often by composting done at the appropriate time. First, the soil is fed, which in turn feeds the plants, which will eventually feed the animals, which will become food for humans (MAPAQ, 2000).

Soil that is vitally abundant and rich is the result of farmers who have maintained a humus and good soil structure to avoid soil breakdown and erosion. Organic farming practices largely contribute to reducing pollution which is sometimes a by-product of farming (MAPAQ, 2000).

While it protects the soil, organic farming also results in foods that, in the opinion of many, are better tasting and more healthy than mass produced farm products (Dufresne, 2001).

It is a well known fact that the effect of modern farming practices on the environment "are noticeable by way of water pollution, soil breakdown and the presence of pesticides in the ecosystem" (Boutin, 2001).

So, why eat organically grown foods? Because, contrary to the opinion of the farming industry, the soil is not just a base for growing plants; it is a living organism that gives life to the extent that we allow it to. The use of chemical fertilisers and pesticides kills the soil by destroying its micro-fauna, micro-flora and enzymes by altering its natural chemical state. The soil is then structurally and texturally modified: it loses its cohesion, breaks down and becomes extremely sensitive to erosion, to seepage and to the draining of its nutrients. True, legumes, cereals, fruits and vegetables continue to grow, but out of a soil that is depleted. They are by-products of the pesticides with which they were sprayed and of the fertilisers spread on the ground; they are no more than what the soil had to offer.

This loss of vitality makes its way down the food chain: plants lose their vitality... and so on, down to the naïve, uninformed, consenting bipeds that we are. Of course we eat these products, but they lack vital organisms that did not survive all the chemical treatments they underwent.

According to researchers at *The Land Institute*, there is nothing more sacred than the tie that binds humans to the earth that feeds them (Mathieu, 2001), and they are absolutely right.

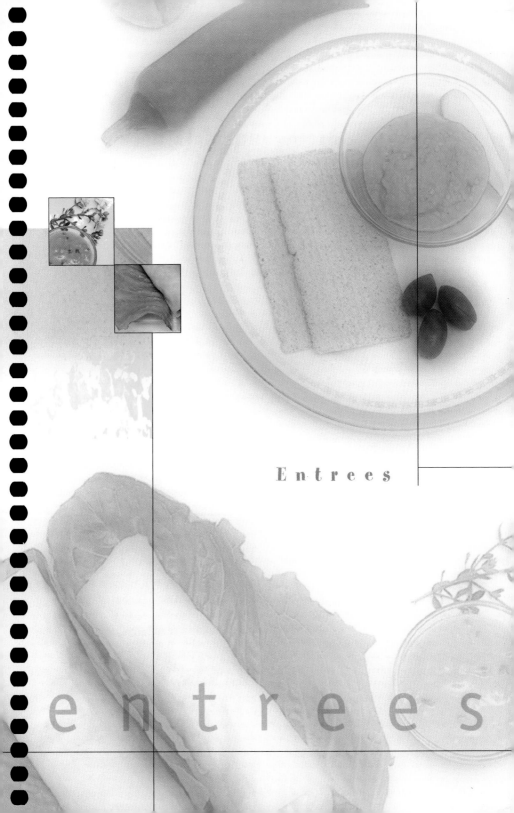

Entrees

entrees

Melitzanosalata with Miso
(pureed eggplant)

This is a simple and tasteful way to prepare eggplant, a vegetable that everyone loves to look at but wonders how to use it, other than in moussaka and ratatouille. The puree, that the French prefer to name "eggplant caviar", is a Greek dish with endless varieties throughout the Mediterranean. Eggplant has been a staple in Asia for 2500 years and is originally a fruit from a plant native to India. It helps to lower cholesterol (Chevalier, 1997). It is also known to be a diuretic and a laxative.

Pureed eggplant should be served fresh, garnished with olives (optional) on plain or toasted bread, biscotti or crackers, or with fresh vegetables.

For 6 to 8 persons
Preparation time: 15 minutes, once the eggplant is cooked.
Cooking time: 1 hour

Ingredients:
1 medium to large eggplant
2 tbsp lemon juice (1/2 lemon)
3 garlic cloves
1 tbsp chopped parsley
1 tbsp miso
3 tbsp olive oil

Preparation:
Pierce the eggplant two or three times with a fork so that it doesn't explode during the baking process. Bake it in the oven, as is, at 375° F (190° C) for 1 hour or until the skin wrinkles and begins to brown.

Cut the eggplant in half lengthwise, scoop out the flesh with a spoon, being careful not to tear the skin. Puree the eggplant with the other ingredients and refrigerate the mixture.

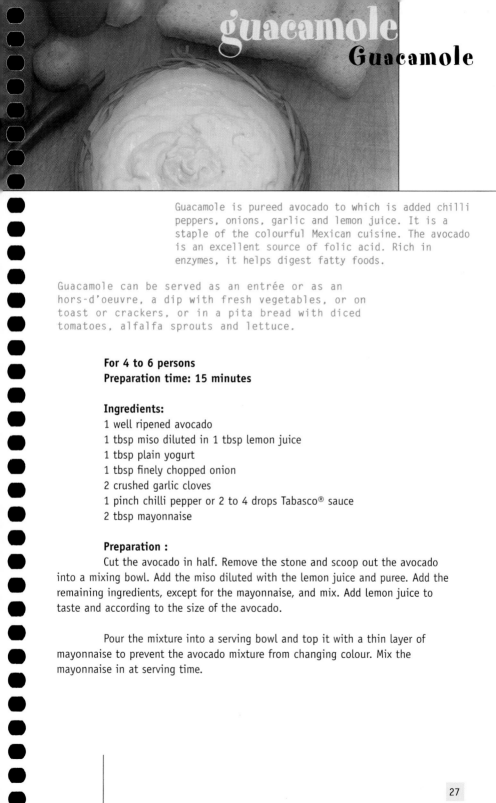

Guacamole is pureed avocado to which is added chilli peppers, onions, garlic and lemon juice. It is a staple of the colourful Mexican cuisine. The avocado is an excellent source of folic acid. Rich in enzymes, it helps digest fatty foods.

Guacamole can be served as an entrée or as an hors-d'oeuvre, a dip with fresh vegetables, or on toast or crackers, or in a pita bread with diced tomatoes, alfalfa sprouts and lettuce.

For 4 to 6 persons
Preparation time: 15 minutes

Ingredients:
1 well ripened avocado
1 tbsp miso diluted in 1 tbsp lemon juice
1 tbsp plain yogurt
1 tbsp finely chopped onion
2 crushed garlic cloves
1 pinch chilli pepper or 2 to 4 drops Tabasco® sauce
2 tbsp mayonnaise

Preparation :
Cut the avocado in half. Remove the stone and scoop out the avocado into a mixing bowl. Add the miso diluted with the lemon juice and puree. Add the remaining ingredients, except for the mayonnaise, and mix. Add lemon juice to taste and according to the size of the avocado.

Pour the mixture into a serving bowl and top it with a thin layer of mayonnaise to prevent the avocado mixture from changing colour. Mix the mayonnaise in at serving time.

miso sushi

Miso Sushi

Sushi is pleasing to the eye and easy to prepare in all its varieties. The following recipe is a simple vegetarian version which can be varied in endless ways by adding small Matane shrimps, smoked salmon strips, matchstick carrot pieces, shiitake mushrooms, lacto-fermented vegetables and so on.

Sushi goes well with marinated ginger and Tamari or shoyu lightly diluted with water. It can be served as an hors-d'oeuvres or as an entree, or as a side dish with Japanese salmon steak for example.

For 4 persons
Yield: 4 sushi rolls
Preparation time: 30 minutes

Ingredients:
I cup pearl or short grain rice (calrose, arborio or sushi rice)
2 eggs
3 tbsp rice vinegar
3 tbsp miso
1 ripe avocado cut in strips
1 green onion cut in strips
4 nori leaves (algae sheets for sushi)

Preparation :
Bring 1 3/4 cups water to a boil, add the rice and cook until the rice has absorbed all the water. Meanwhile, beat the eggs lightly, cook them in a pan with some butter, let them cool and cut them in strips. Mix the rice vinegar and miso together and add to the cooked rice.

Lay one nori sheet on a small sushi mat or on a damp cloth. With a spoon, evenly spread a thin layer of rice, leaving a 3 cm border without rice at the top of the sheet. Moisten the top edge with water. At the bottom of the sheet, parallel to the top border, place a few strips of egg, avocado and green onion. With the small mat or damp cloth, roll up the nori sheet to the top edge. Refrigerate the rolls.

To serve the rolls, dip a knife in a mix of water and vinegar to avoid sticking and cut the rolls into eight small portions.

Vegetarian Pâté

Yield: 24 small rectangular pâtés
Preparation time: 45 minutes
Cooking time: 55 minutes

Ingredients :
1 lb firm tofu, crumbled by hand
2 cups lightly toasted and coarsely chopped sunflower seeds
1 cup whole wheat flour
1/2 cup torula or engevita yeast
3/4 cup wheat germ
2 tbsp allspice or croquettes spices (p. 51)
2 onions finely chopped
2 medium patatoes grated
1 grated carrot
1 celery stalk finely chopped
3 crushed garlic cloves
1/2 cup olive oil
1 cup white wine
1 1/4 cup water
2 tbsp lemon juice
6 tbsp miso diluted in 1/2 cup lukewarm water

Preparation :
Combine all ingredients in the order they are listed. Coat two 8 X 10 inch rectangular baking pans with oil or butter. Pour in the mixture and spread it in the pans. Bake at 350° F (180° C) for 55 minutes. Allow to cool at room temperature and refrigerate before cutting the pâté in each pan into twelve rectangles. Wrap each piece in plastic wrap and freeze.

This vegetarian pâté recipe is a true find. Tofu provides a smooth texture while miso, toasted sunflower seeds and yeast lend the taste so essential in a pâté.

Vegetarian pâté is best served cold on fresh or toasted bread, crackers or in a sandwich.

Spring Rolls

Spring rolls, more easily digested than imperial rolls and other egg rolls as they are not deep fried, appear in most south west Asian cooking. This recipe is a vegetarian version of spring rolls to which can be added 1/2 cup of cooked shrimp or cooked diced chicken.

For 6 persons
Yield: 12 rolls
Preparation time: 45 minutes

Ingredients:
12 rice sheets
12 lettuce leaves

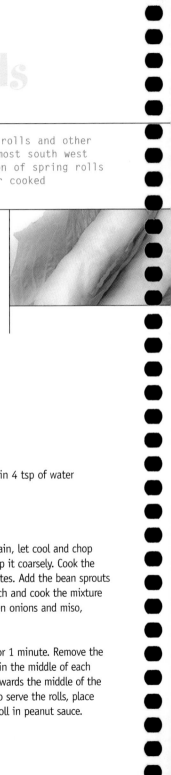

Filling:
4 oz rice vermicelli
1 egg
4 oz chopped mushrooms
3 cloves of garlic chopped
1 tbsp butter
7 oz bean sprouts chopped
2 tsp nuoc man or nampla (fermented fish sauce)
1 tsp honey
1 tsp corn starch (or 1/2 tsp arrow-root starch) diluted in 4 tsp of water
2 green onions chopped
2 tbsp miso diluted in 1 tbsp of water

Preparation :
Immerse the vermicelli in boiling water for 5 minutes. Drain, let cool and chop coarsely. Beat the egg gently, cook it in some of the butter and chop it coarsely. Cook the mushrooms and garlic gently in the remaining butter for a few minutes. Add the bean sprouts and cook 2 minutes longer. Add the nuoc man, honey and corn starch and cook the mixture until thickened. Remove from heat and add the vermicelli, egg, green onions and miso, and mix well.

Soak each rice sheet in a large bowl of lukewarm water for 1 minute. Remove the sheet from the water and lay it on a board. Place 2 tbsp of garnish in the middle of each sheet and begin to roll the sheet 1 1/2 turns, then fold the sides towards the middle of the garnish, and finish rolling up the sheet. Repeat for all rice sheets. To serve the rolls, place each roll on a lettuce leaf, guests will roll it up before dipping the roll in peanut sauce. Serve at room temperature.

Peanut Sauce

Yield: 1 cup (250 ml) for 12 spring rolls
Preparation time: 10 minutes

Ingredients :
2 tbsp finely chopped onion
1/2 cup peanut butter
1 tbsp honey
1 tbsp nuoc man or nampla (fermented fish sauce)
1 cup lukewarm water
1 tsp Dijon mustard or mustard seeds
1/4 to 1/2 tsp dried chili pepper or fresh chopped habanero pepper
2 tbsp corn starch (or 1 tbsp arrow-root starch) mixed in 1/4 cup of water
2 tbsp miso diluted in 1 tbsp hot water

Preparation :
In a small pot or pan, mix all ingredients together except for the cornstarch and miso mixtures. Cook over low heat to the boiling point. Add the corn starch mixed with the water. Cook until the sauce thickens; it can become quite thick. Remove from heat and stir in the diluted miso.

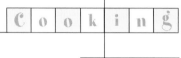

Cooking Tips

People who suffer from allergies or food intolerance should consume miso with the foods causing the allergy. For example, to counter an allergy to bread, add miso to the dish being served.

To counter food intolerance, let the food rest once miso has been added to it. This will allow the enzymes to hydrolyse the protein and sugar causing the intolerance.

Broths and Soups

broths
and soups

simple and delicious
miso broth

Simple and Delicious
Miso Broth

Yield: 1 cup (250 ml)
Preparation time: 5 minutes

Ingredients :
1 tsp miso
1 cup hot water
1 pinch chopped green onion
1 pinch fresh parsley

Preparation :
Dilute the miso in some of the hot water then fill the cup with the remaining water. Add the chopped green onion and parsley.

This energy-enhancing broth is a great substitute for coffee and tea. This is much the way the Japanese have it, in the morning, adding seaweed, mushrooms and tofu.

Miso Consommé

The "miso" version of consommé can be taken as is, used as
a base for preparing soup or added to any recipe calling for
a broth. With the slight addition of red wine it becomes an
excellent bouillon for Chinese fondue.

Yield: 2 1/2 cup (625 ml)
Preparation time: 10 minutes
Cooking time: 45 minutes

Ingredients :
1 tbsp oil
1 onion quartered
1 carrot quartered
1 celery stalk coarsely chopped
2 to 5 cloves of garlic halved
2 whole cloves
3 bay leaves
6 whole grains of pepper
1/2 tsp of thyme
4 cups of water
2 tbsp miso diluted in 1/4 cup of hot water
1 sprig of parsley finely chopped

Preparation :
Heat the oil in a pan and sauté all the ingredients except for the miso,
water and parsley. Cook at low heat for 5 minutes. Add the water, cover and let
simmer for 30 minutes. Remove from heat and strain the mixture. Mix in the diluted
miso. Add the chopped parsley and serve hot.

Cream of Leek Soup

Cream of leek soup, also called "vichyssoise", is a classic French cuisine dish. It is included in the recipes of the "Académie culinaire de France".

Serves 6 persons
Preparation time: 30 minutes
Cooking time: 30 minutes

Ingredients :
2 tbsp butter
4 medium leeks chopped
1 medium onion chopped
2 cloves of garlic chopped
4 medium potatoes peeled and cut into cubes
2 stalks of celery cut in strips
1/2 tsp chervil
1/2 tsp marjoram
2 cups water

1 cup of milk
3 tbsp miso diluted in 1/4 cup of hot water
2 tbsp chives or green onions finely chopped
A few garlic croutons

Preparation :
In a cooking pan, melt the butter and cook the leek, onion and garlic together for 5 minutes stirring constantly. Add the potatoes, celery, chervil, marjoram and half the water. Cover and let simmer for 25 minutes or until the vegetables are tender. Let cool for 15 minutes.

Place the mixture in a food processor and puree. Before serving, pour the mixture back into the cooking pan and add the milk and the remaining water. Bring to a boil beating constantly. Remove from heat and add the miso.

Pour the soup in serving bowls and top with a few croutons and chives or green onions, and serve hot. For a carrot soup, substitute the leeks for 2 cups of grated carrots.

Oriental Meal Soup

A healthy, low in calorie, easy-to-prepare meal in a bowl that is ideal for fall, winter and springtime lunches.

Serves 4 to 6 persons
Yield: 10 cups (2.5 litres)
Preparation time: 20 minutes

Ingredients :
8 cups chicken broth
1/2 cup cooked shrimps or 1 tbsp dried shrimps
1/2 cup cooked chicken pieces
A few mushrooms (shiitake or other) or algae (hijiki or other) chopped
2 tbsp dried onion
1/2 cup bean sprouts
1 stalk of celery chopped
1 cup of cabbage cut in strips
1/2 cup spinach chopped
1 tbsp nuoc man (fermented fish sauce)
1/2 tsp dried chilli pepper
4 oz rice vermicelli
3 tbsp miso diluted in 2 tbsp hot water
2 green onions chopped
1 tbsp parsley chopped or cut

Preparation :
In a pot, mix all ingredients except for the last four. Bring to a boil, let simmer for 15 minutes and remove from heat. Add the miso. Meanwhile, soak the rice vermicelli in boiling water for 5 minutes then drain.

Divide the rice vermicelli into the individual serving bowls, top each portion with soup, garnish with chopped green onion and parsley and serve.

Vegetarian Goulash

Goulash is a traditional Hungarian dish, usually prepared with morsels of beef. Its spicy taste comes from paprika, a main condiment of the Hungarian cuisine. This is a meatless adaptation that may be served as soup or as a meal, depending on what is added to lend consistency: tofu, seitan (wheat gluten), tempeh, etc.

Goulash may also be served with rice, bulgur or potatoes.

For 6 persons
Preparation time:
10 minutes
Cooking time:
40 minutes

Ingredients :
2 tbsp olive oil
4 onions cut in strips
1 lb. extra firm tofu cut in 1 cm^3
1 tbsp butter
1 tbsp olive oil
1 tbsp flour
1 tsp paprika
2 or 3 tomatoes diced
1 red pepper cut in strips
4 cups of water
3 tbsp miso mixed with some juices from cooking
2 tbsp plain yogurt per bowl of soup

Preparation :
Heat the oil and butter in a pot and cook the onion for ten minutes. Meanwhile, in a pan, cook the tofu in the hot oil and butter until it is golden on all sides (approx. 10 minutes), and remove from heat.

In the pot containing the onion, add the flour, mix well and cook for one minute. Add the paprika, tomatoes, pepper and water. Let simmer for 25 minutes. Add the tofu. Heat for 2 minutes or more, add the miso and serve hot in soup bowls or deep dishes. Gently add two tbsp plain yogurt to each bowl or dish and swirl gently to create a pattern.

Onion Soup au Gratin

Serves 6 persons
Preparation time: 15 minutes
Cooking time: 40 minutes

Another classic French cuisine dish with the addition of miso.

Ingredients :
1 cup herb croutons or 1 slice dry bread
2 tbsp butter
3 medium onions chopped
1/4 cup white wine
2 tbsp flour
6 cups water
1 bay leaf
5 tbsp miso diluted in 1/4 cup hot water
Grated gruyere cheese

Preparation :
If preparing the croutons, cut the slice of bread into cubes and allow them to dry out. Sauté the cubes in 3 tbsp butter and 1 tbsp herbs until they have browned.

In a cooking pan, melt the butter and cook the onions. Reduce the heat and let cook for 10 minutes at low heat, stirring occasionally to glaze the onions. Increase the heat, add the wine, and reduce the mixture to 2/3 quantity. Sprinkle with the flour and mix. Add the water gradually and the bay leaf. Bring to a boil then reduce the heat. Cover and let simmer for 20 minutes. Remove from heat and add the miso.

To serve, pour the soup into oven-proof bowls, top with a few croutons or a slice of bread, sprinkle with cheese and bake at 350° F (180° C) for a few minutes or until golden brown.

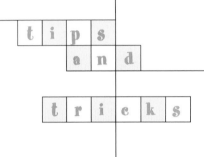

tips and tricks

Adding miso to the
ingredients helps
protect against
pathogenic organisms
such as *E. coli*,
salmonella,
Shygella, etc.

salads

Salads

Greek Style Bean Salad

This salad, adapted from a recipe from a friend, is best served with natural feta cheese, the flavour of which blends well with black olives. Feta is a soft, semi-ripened goat cheese, marinated and preserved in brine.

Serves 4 to 6 persons
Yield: 4 cups
Preparation time: 15 minutes

Ingredients:
1 1/2 cups pre-cooked (19 oz can or 540 ml) rinsed and drained white beans
1 cup feta cheese cubed
1 onion finely chopped
1/2 cup black olives chopped
1/2 cup mustard vinaigrette

Preparation:
Rinse the beans under cold water. Remove the feta cheese from the brine and rinse under cold water if too salty. Combine the ingredients in a salad bowl. Drizzle with Dijon mustard vinaigrette.

Dijon Mustard Vinaigrette

Yield: 1/2 cup (125 ml)
Preparation time: 10 minutes

Ingredients:
2 tbsp miso
3 tbsp white wine
2 tsp Dijon mustard
3 tbsp olive oil
2 cloves of garlic crushed

Preparation:
Combine the miso, wine, mustard and garlic. Pour the oil in a steady stream while mixing.

Fusilli Salad with Tuna

fusilli salad with tuna

Serves 4 to 6 persons
Preparation time: 20 minutes

Ingredients:
3 cups cooked fusilli (small shells or penne)
1 can (6,5 oz or 184 g) tuna
1/2 cup grated cheese (gruyere, emmenthal, strong cheddar)
2 hard-boiled eggs chopped
4 tomatoes cut in 8 pieces
1 tbsp fresh parsley chopped
1/3 cup mayonnaise vinaigrette

Preparation:
Combine all of the ingredients and mix in the mayonnaise vinaigrette.

Fusilli salad is easy to prepare and is a tasty alternative to the traditional macaroni salad. Fusilli is a type of small tortellini or rotini, a short, twist pasta. The salad can be served as a main dish, as an entrée or side dish, or as part of a buffet meal.

Mayonnaise Vinaigrette

Yield: 1/3 cup (85 ml)
Preparation time: 5 minutes

Ingredients:
3 tbsp rice vinegar
3 tbsp miso
3 tbsp mayonnaise

Preparation:
Combine the vinegar and miso.
Add the mayonnaise.

Oriental Salad

This recipe is a healthy
and more complete version
of chop suey. It can be
served as a main dish,
as an entree or as part
of a buffet.

Serves 6 persons
Yield: 6 cups
Preparation time: 20 minutes

Ingredients:
2 celery stalks diced
1/2 cup walnuts coarsely chopped
3 green onions minced
1/2 green pepper and 1/2 red pepper diced
1 cup mushrooms diced
1 package (7 oz or 200 g) bean sprouts
1/2 cup cooked whole rice
Yogurt and honey vinaigrette

Preparation:
Combine all the ingredients in a salad bowl. Add the vinaigrette just
before serving. For each cup of salad, add 2 tbsp yogurt and honey vinaigrette.

Yogurt and Honey Vinaigrette

Yield: 1 cup (250 ml)
Preparation time: 5 minutes

Ingredients:
2 tbsp miso
2 tbsp cider vinegar
3 tbsp plain yogurt
1 tbsp honey
3 cloves garlic minced
3 tbsp olive oil

Preparation:
Combine the miso with the vinegar. Add the yogurt, honey, garlic and,
while combining all the ingredients, pour the oil in a steady stream.

Main Dishes

main dishes

Fresh Tomato Pasta

This is a simple summer pasta recipe in which the tomato holds centre stage. The recipe from Ticino (Swiss-Italian canton), offers a fresh way of serving pasta. The flavour of roka, similar to watercress, blends well with the tomato. But with or without roka, the sauce is delicious. The secret to its taste is fresh tomatoes.

Did you know that the word "tomato" comes from the Aztec *tomatl*?

Serves 4 to 6 persons
Yield: 5 cups (1250 ml)
Preparation time: 10 minutes

Ingredients:
6 ripe medium tomatoes cut into cubes
1 onion cut into cubes
2 tbsp miso diluted in 1 tbsp water
3 garlic cloves crushed
2 tbsp cress finely chopped or 2 tbsp pesto (optional)

Preparation:
Combine the ingredients and set aside for 1/2 hour. Serve at room temperature on warm or hot pasta (spaghetti, spaghettini, fettucini, linguini, tagliatelle, etc.).

Known in most cultures, pasta is easy to prepare and an immediate source of energy. Prepared with a favourite sauce or topping, it is a delicious meal ready in minutes.

The recipe that follows is rich with ingredients but other vegetables can be added according to taste. Serve the sauce hot over spaghetti or other pasta, rice or bulgur, or as a sauce for lasagna. The sauce can be frozen.

Vegetarian Pasta

Serves 10 persons
Yield: 8 cups (2 litres)
Preparation time: 40 minutes
Cooking time: 45 minutes

Ingredients:
4 tbsp oil
1 or 2 onions chopped
3 cloves of garlic chopped
1 cup of firm tofu cubed
1 package of mushrooms sliced
3 carrots grated
1 green pepper and 1 red pepper cubed
1/2 cup green beans cubed
3 stalks of celery cubed
1 can (28 oz or 796 ml) chopped tomatoes
1 can (19 oz or 540 ml) tomato juice
1 small can (5.5 oz or 156 ml) tomato paste
4 tbsp chilli sauce
2 tbsp Worcestershire sauce
1/2 tsp thyme
1 tsp basil
3 tbsp chopped parsley
2 bay leaves
1 pinch chilli pepper
1/2 tsp Cayenne pepper
2 tsp honey
4 tbsp miso diluted in 1/3 cup of water

Preparation:
Heat the oil. Cook the garlic and onion for 2 minutes. Add the tofu and cook for 10 minutes or until lightly browned. Add the remaining ingredients, except for the miso, and mix. Let simmer for 1/2 hour stirring regularly. Remove from heat and add the miso. Serve over pasta.

Ibishyimbo
(kidney beans) with Tomatoes and Sunflower Seeds

As in many countries around the world, the bean is the main source of protein for Central-African farmers. It is a staple of family diets regardless of social status. The recipe suggested here is a traditional Rwandan dish to which the author of this book and friends from Rwanda have succeeded in including miso.

The dish is not unlike the Mexican chili con carne, served with plantains, African spinach, pasta, potatoes, rice, bulgur or pearl barley.

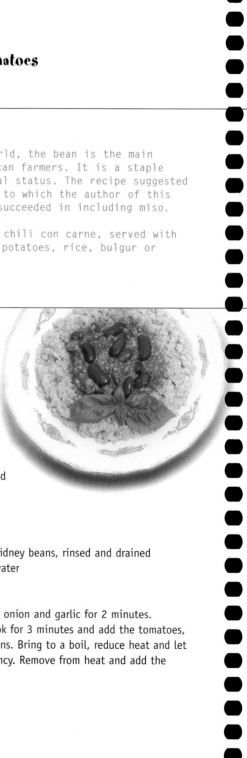

Yield: 4 cups
Preparation time: 30 minutes
Cooking time: 20 minutes

Ingredients:
2 tbsp oil
1 onion chopped
3 cloves of garlic crushed
1/2 cup sunflower seeds ground
4 large tomatoes peeled and crushed
1 tbsp basil
1 tsp oregano
1 tbsp paprika
1/2 tsp hot chilli pepper
1 1/2 cups (19 oz or 540 ml can) kidney beans, rinsed and drained
3 tbsp miso diluted in 2 tbsp hot water

Preparation:
In a pan, heat the oil and cook the onion and garlic for 2 minutes. Add the ground sunflower seeds and mix. Cook for 3 minutes and add the tomatoes, basil, oregano, paprika, chilli pepper and beans. Bring to a boil, reduce heat and let simmer for 10 minutes or to desired consistency. Remove from heat and add the miso. Serve hot.

Japanese Salmon Steak

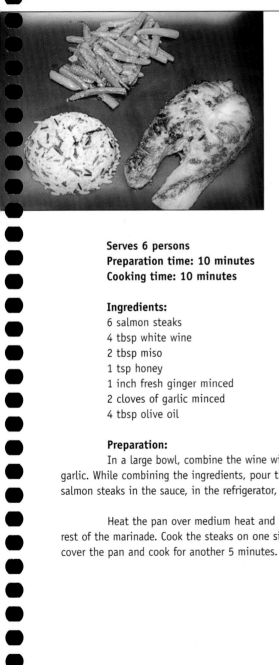

Cooked this way, salmon literally melts in the mouth. The miso marinade tenderises and lends an exquisite taste to the dish. It is an awakening of the taste buds!

This salmon dish can be served with wild rice, green beans with sesame oil and garlic, oriental salad or sushi.

Serves 6 persons
Preparation time: 10 minutes
Cooking time: 10 minutes

Ingredients:
6 salmon steaks
4 tbsp white wine
2 tbsp miso
1 tsp honey
1 inch fresh ginger minced
2 cloves of garlic minced
4 tbsp olive oil

Preparation:
In a large bowl, combine the wine with the miso. Add the honey, ginger and garlic. While combining the ingredients, pour the oil in a steady stream. Marinate the salmon steaks in the sauce, in the refrigerator, for at least 1 hour.

Heat the pan over medium heat and begin cooking the steaks, adding the rest of the marinade. Cook the steaks on one side for 5 minutes, turn the steaks over, cover the pan and cook for another 5 minutes. Serve hot.

Tofu Croquettes with Miso

Yield: 36 1 1/2-in. balls or 12 hamburger patties
Preparation time: 1 hour
Cooking time: 50 minutes at 350° F (180° C)

Ingredients:
1 lb. firm tofu
1 cup cooked sticky rice (short grain, arborio, calrose, etc.)
1/2 cup almonds toasted and ground
1 tbsp olive oil
1 onion finely chopped
1 tbsp chopped parsley
4 cloves of garlic minced
6 tbsp miso
1/2 to 1 cup bread crumbs or enough to bind the mixture
1 1/2 tbsp croquette spices (see recipe below)

2 eggs beaten
1/2 cup bread crumbs
2 tbsp oil

Preparation:
Toast the almonds in olive oil. Grind the almonds with a mortar or in a food processor.

To prepare the bread crumbs: slice the bread into strips and place in the oven at low temperature to dry out, then grind into crumbs (economical in a pre-used and still warm oven).

Drain the tofu well by squeezing it firmly. In a large bowl (or in a food processor), finely crumble the tofu and add the rest of the ingredients, except for the last three, and mix with a wooden spoon. If the mixture is too soft, add bread crumbs.

Roll the mixture into balls or patties, depending on the meal to be served. Dip each ball or patty in the beaten eggs and roll in the bread crumbs. Place on an oiled baking sheet or pan and with a brush, coat with a bit of oil. Bake in a 350° F (180° C) oven for 50 minutes. Turn the balls or patties every 15 minutes. Serve hot or at room temperature.

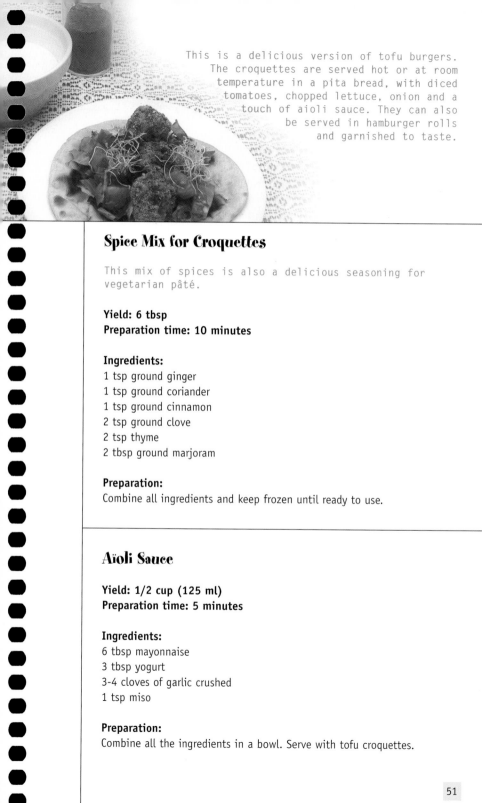

This is a delicious version of tofu burgers. The croquettes are served hot or at room temperature in a pita bread, with diced tomatoes, chopped lettuce, onion and a touch of aioli sauce. They can also be served in hamburger rolls and garnished to taste.

Spice Mix for Croquettes

This mix of spices is also a delicious seasoning for vegetarian pâté.

Yield: 6 tbsp
Preparation time: 10 minutes

Ingredients:
1 tsp ground ginger
1 tsp ground coriander
1 tsp ground cinnamon
2 tsp ground clove
2 tsp thyme
2 tbsp ground marjoram

Preparation:
Combine all ingredients and keep frozen until ready to use.

Aïoli Sauce

Yield: 1/2 cup (125 ml)
Preparation time: 5 minutes

Ingredients:
6 tbsp mayonnaise
3 tbsp yogurt
3-4 cloves of garlic crushed
1 tsp miso

Preparation:
Combine all the ingredients in a bowl. Serve with tofu croquettes.

Singhalese Rice

The combination of aromatic tangy fruit with spicy curry gives Singhalese rice its unique flavour. This recipe calls for apple but a more exotic fruit such as kiwi or mango can be substituted. The rice dish can be served with plain yogurt and dhal.

Serves 6 persons
Preparation time: 15 minutes
Cooking time: 5 minutes

Ingredients:
1 tbsp butter
1 onion chopped
2/3 cup cashew nuts chopped coarsely
1 tbsp curry powder
2 apples cubed
2 cups long grain rice cooked
2 tbsp miso diluted in 2 tbsp hot water
1 cup plain yogurt

Preparation:
Melt the butter and cook the onion and cashew nuts for 2 minutes. Add the curry, apples and rice and mix well. Remove from heat and stir in the miso. Serve hot with yogurt.

Dahl (lentil dish from India)

The secret to the success of Indian cuisine of all kinds lies
in the use of fresh spices which lend a unique taste to grains
and cereals. Spices are usually purchased whole and ground
just before needed. To prepare dhal, it is by far better to
use tomatoes in season, otherwise canned whole tomatoes are
recommended. Dhal can be served with Singhalese rice, yogurt
or simply with brown rice and green vegetables. Bread lovers
can add chapati.

Serves 6 persons
Preparation time: 15 minutes
(excluding soaking of the lentils)
Cooking time: 20 minutes

Ingredients:
1 cup small green lentils
1 tbsp oil
1 onion chopped
2 cloves of garlic chopped
1 tbsp of turmeric
1 tbsp ground ginger
1 tbsp cumin
6 tomatoes each cut in 8 pieces
2 tbsp miso diluted in some cooking juices

Preparation:
Soak the lentils in a 2-litre casserole for approximately 2 hours. Drain and
cover with water. Bring to a boil and cook the lentils for 10 minutes or until they
are easily crushed between the thumb and the index finger. Drain and rinse.
Note: overcooked lentils become pasty.

In a larger casserole, heat the oil and cook the onion for 2 minutes.
Add the turmeric, tomatoes and lentils. Combine and bring to a boil then reduce
heat and let simmer for 5 minutes. Remove from heat and stir in the miso.
Serve hot.

tips and tricks

Adding miso to baked beans enhances digestion and also decreases flatulence.

Coating corn with miso rather than butter will make it more easy to digest and will reduce the risk of flatulence.

Vegetables
and Side Dishes

vegetables
and side dishes

Inspired by Japanese cuisine, these green beans
are served as a vegetable side dish.
They are excellent with Japanese salmon steaks.

Green Beans
with Sesame Oil and Garlic

Serves 4 persons
Yield: 2 cups
Preparation time: 10 minutes
Cooking time: 10 minutes

Ingredients:
2 cups green beans cut in two or three
1 tbsp sesame oil
3 cloves of garlic chopped
1 tbsp miso diluted in 1 tbsp hot water

Preparation:
Pre-cook the green beans in boiling water for 5 minutes. Drain well.

In a cooking pan, heat the sesame oil and cook the garlic for 2 to 3 minutes.
Add the green beans and heat, stirring constantly for 2 minutes. Remove from heat and
stir in the miso. Serve hot.

African Spinach

The original African Spinach dish comes from the Great Lakes region of Africa. In Rwanda, Burundi, Uganda and the Congo, its main ingredient, dodos, a leafy vegetable, is served with manioc (cassava) paste, beans (ibishyimbo) and plantain bananas (ibitoke). As a rule, dodos are cooked in palm oil. The Quebec version is an original, delicious way of preparing spinach.

African spinach can be served as a vegetable side dish with rice, bulgur, polenta, mashed potatoes or plantain bananas.

Serves 4 persons
Preparation time: 15 minutes
Cooking time: 15 minutes

Ingredients:
2 cups water
1 package of spinach (fresh or frozen)
1 onion sliced in rings
3 cloves of garlic minced
2 tbsp olive oil
3 medium tomatoes crushed
1 tbsp peanut butter softened with a bit of crushed tomato
2 tbsp miso diluted in 2 tbsp hot water

Preparation:
Fill a pot with enough water to boil the spinach. If using fresh spinach, wash the leaves and immerse them in the boiling water until soft and slightly reduced in size (maximum 5 minutes). Remove from heat, drain, cool and chop finely.

Heat the oil and glaze the onion and garlic. Add the tomatoes and cook for 10 minutes. Add the peanut butter and spinach and mix well. Remove from heat and stir in the miso. Serve hot.

In the hills of Rwanda and Burundi, the homes of the inhabitants are usually nestled in the middle of their banana field where, essentially, two types of bananas grow: beer bananas used by the wives who compete with one another in the making of urwagwa, and cooking bananas. In between seasons, when seasonal crops are not yet in full production and the previous year's crops are waning, plantain remains a staple needed to sustain life. In this dish, plantain replaces the potato and other starchy foods. It is served with ibishyimbo and spinach or other green vegetables.

Miso Ibitoke
(plantains or cooking bananas)

Serves 4 persons
Preparation time: 10 minutes
Cooking time: 25 minutes

Ingredients:
4 large plantains cut into 2-inch rounds
2 tbsp oil
1 onion finely chopped
3 cloves of garlic crushed
2 cups water
3 stalks of celery finely chopped
3 sprigs of parsley finely chopped
Chilli pepper to taste
2 tbsp miso diluted in 1/4 cup hot water

Preparation:
Peel and wash the plantains. Heat the oil over medium heat and cook the onion and garlic for 2 minutes. Add the plantains, chilli pepper and cook for 4 minutes, stirring constantly.

Add the water and celery and cook over moderate heat for 20 minutes, stirring regularly. Once the plantains are tender when tested, remove from heat and stir the miso. Sprinkle with the chopped parsley. Serve hot.

Here is a delicious and diet-conscious way of eating corn.
The simplicity of the recipe only adds to its appeal. Corn
prepared this way is an ideal side dish. For those who prefer
corn on the cob, miso can be spread on the corn instead of
butter. Served with miso, corn is more easily digested and
less likely to cause flatulence.

Miso Corn

Serves 4 persons
Yield: 2 cups
Preparation time: 10 minutes
Cooking time: 10 minutes

Ingredients:
1 tbsp butter
2 cups fresh corn kernels
1 1/2 tbsp miso diluted in 2 tbsp hot water

Preparation:
Melt the butter over medium heat and add the corn. Cook until tender,
5 to 10 minutes, stirring constantly. Remove from heat and stir in the miso.
Serve hot.

Ratatouille

Preparing ratatouille is certainly a pleasant way to cook fresh vegetables from one's garden.

Serves 6 persons
Preparation time: 20 minutes
Cooking time: 25 minutes

Ingredients:
3 tbsp olive oil
2 onions finely chopped
3 cloves of garlic chopped
1 medium eggplant cut in 1-inch rounds
5 tomatoes cut in quarters
2 or 3 small squash cut in 1/2 inch rounds
2 green peppers cut in wide strips
1 tsp basil
1/2 tsp thyme
2 tbsp miso diluted in a small amount of cooking juices
1 tbsp parsley
Fresh parmesan cheese grated

Preparation:
Heat the oil and brown the onion and garlic. Add the eggplant and tomatoes and cook 4 to 5 minutes, stirring occasionally. Add the squash, peppers and seasonings. Let simmer, stirring occasionally until the vegetables are tender, about 20 minutes. Remove from heat and stir in the miso. Sprinkle with parsley and parmesan. Serve hot.

sauces and vinaigrettes

Sauces and Vinaigrettes

Dijon Mustard Vinaigrette

Yield: 1/2 cup (125 ml)
Preparation time: 10 minutes

Ingredients:
2 tbsp miso
3 tbsp white wine
2 tsp Dijon mustard
3 tbsp olive oil
2 cloves of garlic crushed

Preparation:
Combine the miso, wine, mustard and garlic. Pour the oil in a steady
stream while mixing.

Mustard is a long-standing and
well-known condiment in cooking
practices around the world. It
dates back as a staple in the
diets of ancient cultures such as
the Egyptians, Greeks and Romans.
In the twelfth century in Avignon,
Pope John XXII actually created
the post of "Mustard First Officer"
whose job it was to oversee the
quality of the mustard served in
the pontiff's palace.

The vinaigrette goes well with the
Greek bean salad and the chickpea
salad. It can also be served with
cubed feta cheese and slices of
fresh tomato lightly sprinkled
with finely chopped onion.

Mayonnaise Vinaigrette

Yield: 1/3 cup (85 ml)
Preparation time: 5 minutes

Ingredients:
3 tbsp rice vinegar
3 tbsp miso
3 tbsp mayonnaise

Preparation:
Combine the vinegar and miso. Add the mayonnaise.

This dressing goes well with pasta or potato salad or simply on slices of fresh tomato sprinkled with chopped fresh parsley.

Yogurt and Honey Vinaigrette

Yield: 1 cup (250 ml)
Preparation time: 5 minutes

Ingredients:
2 tbsp miso
2 tbsp cider vinegar
3 tbsp plain yogurt
1 tbsp honey
3 cloves of garlic chopped
3 tbsp olive oil

This recipe is a perfect combination of tangy and delicate flavours. It is delicious on the Oriental Salad.

Preparation:
Combine the miso and cider vinegar. Add the yogurt, honey, garlic and mix, adding the oil in a steady stream.

Peanut Sauce

A subtly flavoured peanut sauce is the ideal accompaniment
to spring rolls. This one is inspired from a Thai recipe where
it is said that the guests prepare their own spring rolls,
choosing their ingredients from a large plate placed in the
middle of the table.

Yield: 1 cup (250 ml) for 12 spring rolls
Preparation time: 10 minutes

Ingredients:
2 tbsp onion finely chopped
1/2 cup peanut butter
1 tbsp honey
1 tbsp nuoc man or nampla (fermented fish sauce)
1 cup warm water
1 tsp Dijon mustard or mustard seeds
1/4 to 1/2 tsp dried chilli pepper
or fresh habañero pepper chopped
2 tbsp corn starch (or 1 tbsp arrow-root starch) dissolved
in 1/4 cup water
2 tbsp miso diluted in 1 tbsp warm water

Preparation:
Combine all the ingredients in a small pot except for the corn starch and
miso. Cook over low heat to the boiling point. Add the corn starch and stir until
thickened (mixture can be very thick). Remove from heat and stir in the miso.

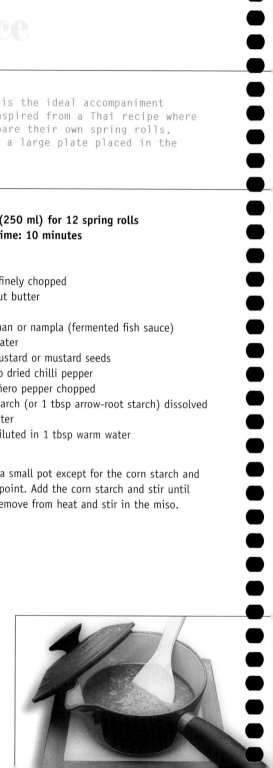

Aïoli Sauce

This sauce, a winner even with the most discriminate eaters, is ideal as a dip for crudités and as a fondue base sauce.

Yield: 1/2 cup (125 ml)
Preparation time: 5 minutes

Ingredients:
6 tbsp mayonnaise
3 tbsp plain yogurt
3 or 4 cloves of garlic crushed
1 tsp miso

Preparation:
Combine all ingredients in a bowl.

Miso Barbecue Sauce

Yield: 1 3/4 cups (435 ml)
Preparation time: 10 minutes
Cooking time: 20 minutes

Ingredients:
1/4 cup olive oil
1 onion finely chopped
3 cloves of garlic chopped
2 tbsp red wine vinegar
1/4 cup ketchup
1 tsp paprika
1/2 cup water
3 tbsp miso diluted in 2 tbsp hot water

This sauce is delicious on "tofu burgers", chicken and meat pies; the addition of miso makes them more easily digestible. The sauce can also be used to coat meat or plantains to be baked in the oven. It makes a wonderful Chinese fondue sauce.

Preparation:
Heat the oil in a small pot and cook the onion and garlic over low heat for 5 minutes. Add the remaining ingredients, except for the miso, bring to a boil and let simmer for 15 minutes. Remove from heat and stir in the miso.

Marinade for Brochettes

Yield: 2/3 cups (170 ml) for 12 brochettes
Preparation time: 10 minutes

Ingredients:
3 tbsp miso diluted in 1/4 cup hot water
1 tbsp honey
1 tbsp fresh ginger finely chopped
3 cloves of garlic crushed
1 green onion finely chopped
3 tbsp olive oil

Preparation:
Combine the miso, honey, ginger, garlic and green onion. Add the olive oil in a steady stream while whisking the ingredients together to a smooth consistency. With a culinary brush, coat the brochettes with the marinade.

Refrigerate the brochettes for 1 to 2 hours before cooking.

This flavourful marinade is ideal as a seasoning for brochettes and also as a meat tenderiser due to protease which enhance digestion.

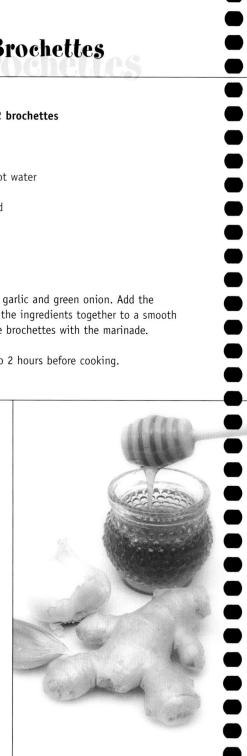

Sweet and Sour Miso Marinade

This marinade is easy to prepare and ideal
for tenderising meat. It lends a wonderful
flavour to various dishes.

Yield: 3/4 cups (185 ml)
Preparation time: 10 minutes

Ingredients:
3 tbsp miso
3 tbsp lemon juice
2 tbsp honey
3 cloves of garlic crushed and minced
5 tbsp olive oil.

Preparation:
Combine the miso, lemon juice, honey and garlic. Add the olive oil in
a steady stream while stirring the ingredients.

Suggestion:
Marinate tofu cubes, sausage, meat or fish for 1/2 hour to 1 hour.
Depending on the dish, bake in the oven or cook in a pan, coating with the
leftover marinade.

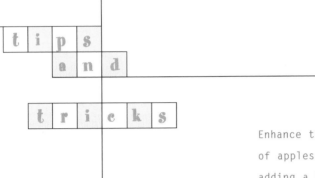

tips and tricks

Enhance the flavour
of applesauce by
adding a bit of
miso after cooking.

When baking bread,
replace salt with
miso containing
amylase (found
in some commercial
brands of flour)
to enhance the
dough-rising
process.

other recipes

Other Useful Recipes

Broth for Infants

Preparation time: 5 minutes

Ingredients:
1/2 tsp miso diluted in a small amount of boiling water
1 cup water

Preparation:
Bring the water to a boil. Remove from heat and add the miso diluted in water. Let stand for a few minutes. Take 2 tbsp from the surface of the mixture and combine with milk, juice, cereal or boiled water. The broth can be given to infants 3 to 4 times daily.

The broth can be given to infants 4 months of age or older. It improves digestion and as such, weaning. It can also be used to counter dehydration due to diarrhea.

Soy Milk

Increasingly present on store shelves, soy milk is a good substitute for dairy milk as it is rich in protein, vitamins and trace elements. It is also more easily digested. The following recipe is easy to prepare. The protein content of this recipe can be increased by adding 1 cup of rice milk (found in natural food stores) for each cup of soy milk. The milk can also be made with 1 cup of soy and 1 1/2 cups of rice. The protein from the rice completes the soy protein content. It is important to use a variety of soy that is appropriate for the recipe, soy that is rich in protein and low in oil.

Yield: 5 to 6 cups (1,25 to 1,5 litres)
Preparation time: 15 minutes
Cooking time: 25 minutes

Ingredients:
2 cups organic dry soy
8 cups water

Preparation:
Clean the soy thoroughly and soak in water overnight. The following morning, drain and rinse the soy. Reduce the soy to a paste using a mortar, or in a food processor, using half the soy at a time, combined with 1 cup of water. Transfer the mixture to a thick-based pan, pour in the remaining water and mix well. Cook over medium heat for 20 minutes from the time the mixture begins to boil. Stir regularly. Because the milk will tend to foam up, stir constantly and reduce the heat if necessary to avoid the mixture spilling over the sides of the pan. Allow the mixture to cool, then filter through a clean cloth. Press the cloth by hand and extract the maximum amount of liquid.

To enhance flavour and the nutritive value of the milk, add maple syrup, a bit of mild almond extract and 1 tbsp dry yeast. The milk will keep well in the refrigerator for 5 days.

Soy Yogurt

Making soy yogurt is simple with soy milk. Fermentation enhances the digestion of soy milk. Soy yogurt, like traditional yogurt, contains lactobacilli, probiotic bacteria capable of preventing and treating various germ infections.

To add flavour to yogurt and to increase its nutritive value, once fermented, include crushed or cut up fruit, fruit juice, honey or maple syrup.

Yield: 5 cups (1,25 litres)
Preparation time: 5 minutes
Cooking time: 25 minutes

Ingredients:
5 cups soy milk
4 to 5 tbsp fresh milk yogurt or 1 sachet yogurt culture

Preparation:
Clean a 2-litre thermos well and rinse in boiling water.

Bring the soy to room temperature, 113° F (45° C), add the yogurt and mix well. Pour the mixture into a thermos and seal air tight. Let sit for 5 hours. The milk will have curdled and the soy yogurt will be ready. Place the yogurt in a clean container and refrigerate. Soy yogurt keeps well for 1 to 2 weeks in the refrigerator.

Germination

Germination greatly increases the nutritive value of beans, and enhances flavour and digestion. Like miso, bean sprouts are rich in enzymes, needed during the winter months when seasonal vegetables are not available. Almost any bean can be germinated - soy, wheat, alfalfa, mustard, onion, etc. Germinating time varies according to the bean.

The mungo bean plays an important role in the cooking habits of a number of Asian countries. The mungo bean sprout is the basic ingredient in chop suey. Note that the expression "germinated bean" is not accurate; it is not a question of beans but of the sprouts themselves.

Mungo sprouts can be eaten in a salad (Oriental Salad), or in a variety of other dishes such as Oriental Soup, Spring Rolls, etc. The mungo sprout is an excellent source of folic acid.

Ingredients:
1/4 cup dry mungo beans (preferably organically grown)
1 litre of water

Preparation:
Clean the beans well. In a bowl containing 1 to 2 litres of water, soak the beans overnight. The following day, drain, rinse and cover the container with a clean cloth secured with an elastic band. With one hand on the cloth, invert the container onto a plate. If the container is transparent, place it in a dark location to avoid the light turning the sprouts green.

Rinse the sprouts under fresh water twice a day for 5 days, preferably, mornings and evenings. The germination is then complete.

Making Pasta:
Simple and Easy

Good quality pasta is made from a variety of hard wheat, durum wheat, with a high protein content, rich in gluten and lower in starch than soft wheat. Pasta can be made from other types of flour: soft wheat, a mix of hard and soft wheat, buckwheat, rice or corn (less common). It can be combined with other ingredients: soy flour, mungo flour, vegetables (spinach, tomato, carrot, beet, etc,), herbs and spices.

Serves 6 to 8 persons
Preparation time: 20 minutes
Cooking time: 3 to 5 minutes

Ingredients:
3 cups whole wheat flour
1 tsp salt
4 whole eggs
1 tbsp oil
Water, if necessary

Preparation:

Sift the flour and salt together in a mixing bowl. Form a well in the middle of the flour and add the eggs and oil. With a fork, beat the eggs in the oil, adding the flour on the edges progressively. Form a ball and knead by hand for 10 minutes, until the dough is smooth. Add a bit of flour if the dough is sticky or a bit of cold water if it is too dry or hard to knead. Divide the dough in four portions and let sit for 30 minutes or so.

To make the pasta, dust the work surface with flour and roll out each portion into a very thin square shape. Dust the flattened dough with flour, roll it up and cut the roll into small strips in the desired width and then unroll. Note: it is certainly easier to prepare pasta with a pasta machine.

Hang the fresh pasta on a string or spread on a cloth to dry for about an hour before cooking.

To cook the pasta, fill a large pot 3/4 full with water. Bring the water to a full boil and cook the pasta for 3 to 5 minutes. Drain and serve hot topped with a sauce of choice.

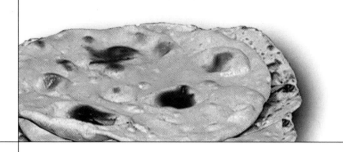

Chapati (unleavened bread)

Pita in the Middle-East, tortilla in Mexico or chapati in India, these are all forms of easy-to-prepare unleavened bread.

Chapati is served hot or cold, stuffed with tofu balls or croquettes with diced tomato, chopped lettuce and aïoli sauce. Chapati can also be served with sprouts, tomato and sunflower seeds or with dhal.

Yield: 10 to 12 chapati
Preparation time: 20 minutes
Cooking time: 20 minutes

Ingredients:
3 cups whole wheat flour
1 cup warm water
A small amount of oil or butter

Preparation:
Sift the flour into a bowl, form a well and pour in the water. Combine the flour and water to form a ball. Knead the dough and keep folding it over for 10 to 15 minutes until it is smooth. Add flour while kneading, a pinch at a time, until the dough is no longer sticky to the touch. It is important not to add too much flour.

Divide the dough into 10 or 12 equal portion balls. Sprinkle flour on the work surface. Roll out each ball with a rolling pin to form a thin round 6-inch circle.

At medium to high heat, in an ungreased pan, cook each bread portion for about 2 minutes on each side; be careful not to burn the bread. When cooked, coat each chapati with a bit of oil or butter.

Healthy Baked Beans with no Fat

This is a healthy version of the traditional "home-baked beans". They are more easily digested, contain no fat and are almost flatulence proof. Adding miso to the dish after cooking makes the beans more digestible, even for people who do not digest beans well.

Serves 8 persons
Preparation time: 10 minutes
Cooking time: 10 hours

Ingredients:
1 lb or 2 cups white dry beans
1/2 cup brown sugar
1/4 cup molasses
2 whole cloves of garlic unpeeled
1 onion cut in half
1/2 tsp dry mustard
1/2 cup miso diluted in 1/2 cup hot water

Preparation:
In a casserole or roasting pan, combine all of the ingredients except for the miso. Add enough water to cover the ingredients by 1/2 inch for a roasting pan and 1 inch for a casserole pan. Bake at 250° F (120° C) overnight (10 hours). Add the miso and serve hot.

Most cases of milk intolerance are due to a deficiency in lactase, the enzyme that breaks down the lactose into glucose and galactose. Miso contains lactase. Also, adding miso to milk and allowing it to ferment for a few hours makes milk more easy to digest for persons who usually cannot digest or tolerate milk.

More Digestible Milk

Yield: 1 litre
Preparation time: 5 minutes
Fermentation time: 4 hours

Ingredients:
1 litre of milk
1 level tbsp of miso

Preparation:
Heat the milk to 113° F (45° C). Add the miso and mix well with a kitchen whisk.

Pour the milk into a 2-litre thermos or let it sit in the pot and place the pot in the oven for 4 hours with the oven light on.

Check for tolerance by drinking a small portion of milk at a time.

Sauerkraut
and Lacto-Fermentation

Sauerkraut is a traditional German or Alsatian dish prepared
with lacto-fermented cabbage. However, according to historians,
sauerkraut originated in China, to feed hundreds of thousands of
workers on the Great Wall (Aubert, 1985). In any event, sauerkraut
is popular in France, Germany, Russia, Bulgaria, Poland, China,
Korea, Indonesia, etc.

Tests have shown that pathogenic bacteria are killed or arrested
in lacto-fermented products. Lacto-fermentation reduces the spread
of various infectious diseases: for one, lactic acid produced from
fermentation inhibits the growth of pathogenic micro-organisms;
fermentation also produces antibacterial and antibiotic substances
(Aubert, 1985), lactobacilli and enzymes.

Sauerkraut, rich in lactobacilli, is an important source of
vitamin C making it an ideal food during the winter months.
During the Middle Ages and the Renaissance period, for prolonged
ocean trips, eating sauerkraut was effective in preventing scurvy,
an illness due to a vitamin C deficiency.

In the method of fermentation suggested here, cabbage can be
replaced or combined with carrots, turnip, onions, radish slices,
and many other vegetables. Whatever the recipe, the principle
for all lacto-fermented vegetables is the same: vegetables, cut
or whole, must soak in their juice or in lightly salted water
for the lactic or anaerobic fermentation to develop, the reason
for weighing down the plate over the vegetables with a stone
during fermentation (Aubert, 1985).

Sauerkraut can be served hot or cold. After fermentation,
the juices can also be consumed.

Preparation time: 30 minutes
Fermentation time: 9 to 14 days

Ingredients:
6 to 7 lb cabbage cut into narrow strips (2 to 3 cabbages)
5 tbsp sea salt
2 tbsp juniper berries

Preparation:
Wash the cabbage, core and cut into quarters, reserving a few whole leaves.
Slice the cabbage in thin strips and combine with salt and juniper berries.

Place a few cabbage leaves on the bottom of the jar and pour in the cabbage
mixture, salt and juniper berries, packing down firmly. Cover with cabbage leaves.

Cover with a cloth, pressing the edges down between the mixture and the
sides of the jar. Invert a heavy plate, slightly smaller in diameter than the jar, over the
mixture. Place a heavy stone or a sealed container filled with 1 or 2 litres of water on
the plate. If using a stone, it must be smooth, clean and sterilised. Cover the jar with
clear plastic wrap and secure with an elastic. After a few days, the liquid should cover
the mixture by 4 to 6 inches; if not, increase the weight of the stone or container of
water. Let ferment for 9 to 14 days, at room temperature, until bubbles no longer pop
up at the surface. Skim the foam off the top of the mixture daily.

After fermentation, the sauerkraut can be preserved in the same jar, in a
cool place, preferably in the refrigerator, for 3 to 4 months.

Bibliography

ARAI, Y., M. UEHARA, Y. SATO, M. KIMIRA, A. EBOSHIDA, H. ADLERCREUTZ et S. WATANABE. *Comparison of isoflavones among dietary intake, plasma concentration and urinary excretion for accurate estimation of phytoestrogen intake*, Journal of Epidemiology, mars 2000, 10 (2), 127-135.

ARIMA, Y., et T. UOZUMI. *A new method for estimation of the mycellium weight in koji*, Agr. Biol. Chem., vol. 31, 1967, p. 119-123.

AUBERT, Claude. *Les aliments fermentés traditionnels, une richesse méconnue*, Éditions Terre Vivante, Paris, 1985, p. 32-228.

BAILEY, James E., et David F. OLLIS. *Biochemical Engineering Fundamentals, Isolation and Utilization of enzymes*, chap. 4, McGraw-Hill, 1977, p. 155-220.

BIENVENIDO, O. *Rice: chemistry and technology, American association of cereal*, Min., 1985, 645 p.

BLAIN, J. A. *Industrial enzyme production, « The filamentous fungi »*, Industrial Mycology, vol. I, Edward Arnold Ltd., Great Britain, 1975, p. 193-211.

BOUTIN, Denis. « *Agriculture et environnement : la difficile cohabitation* », L'AGORA, vol. 8 no 3, juin-juillet 2001, p. 15-16.

CHEVALIER, Andrew. *Encyclopédie des plantes médicinales*, Sélection du Reader's Digest, Montréal, 1997, 336 p.

CYR, Josiane. « *Aliments acides, aliments alcalins* », section Santé du Dimanche Magazine, cahier B, journal Le Soleil, 14 novembre 1999, p. 3.

CYR, Josiane. « *Les arbres en supplément* », Les Conseils de Josiane, La Bonne Table, cahier I, journal Le Soleil, 21 avril 2001, p. 7.

CYR, Josiane. « *Pourquoi consommer des sources de protéines* », Les Conseils de Josiane, La Bonne Table, cahier G, journal Le Soleil, 30 juin 2001, p. 6.

CYR, Josiane. « *Menu du futur : fini les viandes et les produits laitiers* », Les conseils de Josiane, La Bonne Table, cahier I, journal Le Soleil, 29 janvier 2000, p. 8.

CYR, Josiane. « *Eau pétillante sucrée : pas si naturelle* », Les Conseils de Josiane, La Bonne Table, cahier I, journal Le Soleil, 27 janvier 2001, p. 8.

D'AMICO, Serge, and others. *L'Encyclopédie visuelle des aliments*, Les Éditions Québec/Amérique, Montréal, 1996, 688 p.

DUFRESNE, Jacques. « *L'agriculture à l'heure de la complexité* », L'AGORA, vol. 8 no 3, juin-juillet 2001, p. 5-8.

EBINE, H. *Industrialization of indigenous fermented foods*, Marcel Dekker Inc., New York, 1989, p. 89-125.

GAGNON, Yves. « Le Bio, une voie de contournement des OGM », *Bio-Bulle, le magazine du bio québécois*, Numéro 31, Spécial OGM, juin 2001, p. 30-34.

GOTOH, T., K. YAMADA, A. ITO, H. YIN, T. KATAOKA and K. DOHI. *Chemoprevention of N-nitroso-N-methylurea-induced rat mammary cancer by miso and tamoxifen, alone and in combination*, Jpn J. Cancer Res., mai 1998, 89 (5), p. 487-495.

HESSELTINE, C. W., and H. C. WANG. *Fermented Soybean food products,* Develop. Ind. Microbiol., 1972, p. 389-417.

HIROTA, A, S. TAKI, S. KAWAII, M. YANO and N. ABE. *1,1-Dipheny l-2-picrylhydrazyl radical-scavenging compounds from soybean miso and antiproliferative activity of isoflavones from soybean miso toward the cancer cell lines,* Biosc Biotechnol Biochem, 64 (5), mai 2000, p. 1038-1040.

HIRAYAMA, Takeshi. *Relationship of soybean paste soup intake to gastric cancer risk,* Nutrition and Cancer, 1982, vol. 3, no 4, p. 223-233.

KAMEI, H., T. KOIDE, Y. HASHIMOTO, T. KOJIMA, T. UMEDA and M. HASEGAWA. *Tumor cell growth-inhibiting effect of melanoidind extracted from miso and soy sauce,* Cancer Biother Radiopharm, 12 (6), 1997, p. 405-409.

KANDA, A., Y. HOSHIYAMA and T. KAWAGUSHI. *Association of lifestyle parameters with the prevention of hypertension in elderly Japanese men and women : a four-year follow-up of normotensive subjects,* Asia Pac. J. Public Health, 11 (2), 1999, p. 77-81.

KAUFMAN, P. B., J. A. DUKE, H. BRIELMANN, J. BOIK and J. E. HOYT. *A comparative survey of leguminous plants as source of the isoflavones genistein and daidzein : implications for human nutrition and health,* Journal of Alternative Complement Medecine, Printemps, 3 (1), 1997, p. 7-12.

KLAENHAMMER, Todd R. *Functional Genomics and Rationed Selection of Probiotics,* Montreal International Symposium Proceedings, Probiotics and Health; The Intestinal Microflora, October 13, 2000, p. 1-7.

LACHAPELLE, Judith. « Les OGM pour les nuls », Actuel, cahier B, *La Presse,* 23 juillet 2001, p. 1,3.

LACTAID. *When you suspect lactose intolerance,* Gold Cross Nutritional Supplements, Burnley, 1960, 13 p.

LAMBERT, P. W. *Industrial enzyme production and recovery from filamentous fungi,* The filamentous fungi, vol. 4, 1982, p. 210-237.

LANDRY, Karine. « Pour favoriser la santé cardiaque », *L'Acadie Nouvelle, Nutrition,* 12 mai 2000, p. 28.

LANDRY, Karine. « Le soya, une petite merveille », *L'Acadie Nouvelle,* Nutrition, 27 avril 2001, p. 31.

MAPAQ. *Les aliments certifiés biologiques. Un choix logique,* dépliant publié par le Ministère de l'Agriculture, des pêcheries et de l'alimentation du Québec, 2000.

MASAOKA, Y., H. WATANABE, O. KATOH, A. ITO and K. Dohi. *Effects of miso and NaCl on the development of colonic aberrant crypt foci induced by azoxymethane in F344 rats,* Nutr. Cancer, 32 (1), 1998, p. 25-28.

MATHIEU, Andrée. « *L'agriculture revue et corrigée par Dame Nature* », L'AGORA, vol. 8 no 3, juin-juillet 2001, p. 11-14.

MONETTE, Solange. *Dictionnaire encyclopédique des aliments,* Québec Amérique, Collection Santé/Dictionnaires, Montréal, 1989, 607 p.

MOO-YOUNG, M., A. R. Moreira and R. P. TENGRAY. *Principle of solid-substrate fermentation,* The filamentous fungi, vol. 4, 1982, p. 117-144.

NIWA, Y. *Oxidative injury and its defense system in vivo,* Rinsho Byori, 47 (3), mars 1999, p. 189-209.

OGAWA, A., M. Samoto and K. Takahashi. *Soybean allergens and hypoallergenic soybean products,* J. Nutr. Sci. Vitaminol, Tokyo, 46 (6), décembre 2000, p. 271-279.

PILON, Lise. « Des aliments génétiquement modifiés au supermarché. Que faut-il en penser? », *Bio-Bulle, le magazine du bio québécois,* Numéro 31, Spécial OGM, juin 2001, p. 5-27.

REED, Gerald. *Enzymes in food processing,* Academic Press, New York, 1977, 409 p.

ROY, Claude C. *Probiotics in Diaarheal Disorders in Children: Nominated but not yet Elected,* Montreal International Symposium Proceedings, Probiotics and Health; The intestinal Microflora, october 13, 2000, p.43-47.

SAKURAI, Y., and others. *The constituents of koji,* Agri. Biol. Chem., 41, 1977, p. 619-624.

SÉRALINI, Gilles-Éric. *OGM, le vrai débat.* Dominos, Flammarion, France, 2000, 128 p.

SHURTLEFF, William, and Akiko AOYAGI. *The Book of Miso,* Ten speed press, 1983, 278 p.

SHURTLEFF, William, and Akiko AOYAGI. *Miso Production, The Book of Miso: volume II,* The Soyfood Center, 1983, 80 p.

SMITH, J. E. *Aspergillus,* Plenum Press, New York, 1994, 257 p.

STEINKRAUS, K. H. *Handbook of indigenous fermented foods,* Marcel Dekker Inc., New York, 1983, 116 p.

WALKER, Kenneth-F. « *Le secret de la longévité* », section Santé, cahier C, journal La Presse, 4 mars 2001, p. 4.

WATANABE H., T. UESAKA, S. KIDO, Y. ISHIMURA, K. SHIRAKI, K. KURAMOTO, S. HIRAT, S. SHOJI, O. KATOH and N. FUJIMOTO. *Influence of concomitant miso or NaCl treatment on induction of gastric tumors by N-methyl-N'-nitro-N-nitrosoguanidine in rats,* Oncol. Rep., 6 (5), septembre et octobre 1999, p. 989-993.

YEOH, H. H., F.M. WONG and G. LIM. *Screening for fungal lipase using chromogenic lipid substrates,* Mycologia, vol.78, 1986, p. 298-300.

My Recipes

My Recipes

My Recipes

My Recipes

My Recipes

My Recipes

1 oz = 28 g
4 oz = 112 g
8 oz = 227 g = 1 cup
16 oz = 1 lb = 454 g

3 tsp = 1 tbsp = 15 mL
2 tbsp = 1 oz = 30 mL

	ml	tbsp	tsp	fluid oz
1/4 cup	65	4	12	2
1/3 cup	85	6	18	3
1/2 cup	125	8	24	4
2/3 cup	170	10	30	5
3/4 cup	185	12	36	6
1 cup	250	16	48	8
1 litre	1000			32

Développement économique Canada   Canada Economic Development

Canadä

LAURÉAT 2001
Concours québécois en entrepreneurship

Recipe ideas and adaptation, documentation, research and text by:
Suzanne Dionne, Food Technologist

Documentation, research, text and photography by:
Gilbert Boulay

Translated by:
Suzanne O'Connor, B.A., M.A.

Graphic Design by:
Mireille Vandenberghe, Designer